RESEARCH ON BIPOLARITY AND REFLEXIVITY

RESEARCH ON BIPOLARITY AND REFLEXIVITY

Vladimir A. Lefebvre

With Post Script by Karl Popper

The Edwin Mellen Press
Lewiston•Queenston•Lampeter

Library of Congress Cataloging-in-Publication Data

Lefebvre, Vladimir A.
  Research on bipolarity and reflexivity / Vladimir A. Lefebvre.
    p. cm.
  Includes bibliographical references and indexes.
  ISBN 0-7734-5822-0
  I. Title.

hors série.

A CIP catalog record for this book is available from the British Library.

This book is an enlarged edition of *A Psychological Theory of Bipolarity and Reflexivity* (The Edwin Mellen Press, 1992).

Author photo by of V. Paperny

Copyright © 2006 Vladimir A. Lefebvre

All rights reserved. For information contact

<table>
<tr><td>The Edwin Mellen Press
Box 450
Lewiston, New York
USA 14092-0450</td><td>The Edwin Mellen Press
Box 67
Queenston, Ontario
CANADA L0S 1L0</td></tr>
</table>

The Edwin Mellen Press, Ltd.
Lampeter, Ceredigion, Wales
UNITED KINGDOM SA48 8LT

Printed in the United States of America

To Victorina

TABLE OF CONTENT

ACKNOWLEDGMENT	i
PREFACE TO THE SECOND EDITION	iii
INTRODUCTION TO THE FIRST EDITION	1
PART I. A MODEL OF THE SUBJECT WITH FREE WILL	3
1.1. An Abstract Scheme	3
1.2. Axioms	4
1.3. Deduction of the Analytical Representation of the Subject	6
1.4. The Fixed Points of Operator *Sub*	10
PART II. GENERAL INTERPRETATION	13
2.1. Self-Reflexion, Trend, and Belief	13
2.2. Quantum-Mechanical Analogy	16
2.3. Projecting the State onto a Screen as the Object's Reference	17
PART III. DECISIONS BASED ON THE IMAGE OF THE WORLD	21
3.1. Application of the Model to the Empirical Domain	21
3.2. Categorization of Stimuli	21
3.3. Estimation of Star's Brightness	27
3.4. Altruism	28
PART IV. THE AUTONOMOUS SUBJECT	31
4.1. Four Assumptions on the Autonomous Subject	31
4.2. A Trend to the Self	32
4.3. A Trend to an External Object	33

PART V. DECISIONS BASED ON BELIEF   37

5.1. Pole of Belief, Index of Belief, and Projection of the Subject's State   37
5.2. Social Choice   38
5.3. Categorization in the Bipolar Construct Good-Bad   40
5.4. The Golden Section and Choice of a Point on a Scale   41
5.5 The Golden Section and 'Mere Exposure'   43

PART VI. CATEGORIZATION OF THE SELF AND OTHERS WITH THE HELP
OF BIPOLAR CONSTRUCTS   47

6.1. Historical Excursus   47
6.2. The Experiments of Adams-Webber   48
6.3. A Model of the Process of Self-Evaluation   50
6.4. A Model of the Process of Evaluation of Others   51
6.5. The Probability of Positive Evaluation of Another Person   51
6.6. An Experiment by Grice et al.   52

PART VII. NATURAL GENERATION OF GEOMETRICAL
PROPORTIONS   53

7.1. Historical Excursus   53
7.2. Lockhead's Method   54
7.3. The Golden Section in Generation of Geometrical Proportions as a Result of
Projecting the Subject's State onto a Segment   55

PART VIII. NATURAL GENERATION OF MUSICAL INTERVALS   57

8.1. Historical Excursus   57
8.2. Musical Intervals as Projections of States   64
8.3. Elite Intervals   65
8.4. Formal Deduction of the Just Intonation Set   65
8.5. Major and Minor Triads   68
8.6. Psychological Profiles of Major and Minor   69

8.7. Pelog	72
8.8. Communicative Function of Elite Intervals	73
PART IX. THE SUBJECT WITH IMAGES OF SELF AND OTHER	81
9.1. An Abstract Scheme	81
9.2. Functions Corresponding to the Image of the Group	82
9.3. Analytical Representation of the Subject	83
9.4. The Principle of Maximization of the Ethical Status of the Image of the Self	84
PART X. THE ALGEBRAIC BASIS OF THE MODEL	85
10.1. Gamma-Algebra	85
10.2. Axioms	86
10.3. Algebraic Subject	87
CONCLUSION	89
REFERENCES	93
POST SCRIPT. Text written by Sir Karl Popper.	103
THE ADDITIONAL PART. BIPOLAR CHOICE	105
Introduction	105
1. The Law of Internality in a Logical Scheme of Evolution of Behaviorism	109
2. The Matching Law	111
3. The Attempts to Explain the Matching Law within the Framework of the Science of Behavior	113
4. A Model of the Subject with Internality (MS)	114
5. A Deduction of Theoretical Equation for the Matching Law	118
6. Frequencies as Traces of Probabilities Regulation	119
7. Function of the Uncertain State	122

8. Prediction of Behavioral Patterns	122
9. Animals' Deontological Evaluations	126
10. Sacred Shift	128
11. Conclusion	129
A NOTE TO THE ADDITIONAL PART	131
BIBLIOGRAPHY TO THE ADDITIONAL PART	135
INDEX OF NAMES	139
SUBJECT INDEX	143

ACKNOWLEDGMENT

I would like to express my deep gratitude to Anatol Rapoport who, for many years, has maintained an interest in my research. In particular, I am indebted to him for the empirical orientation of this work. In addition, he has read a few earlier versions of this book and made numerous helpful suggestions.

I am deeply grateful to Sir Karl Popper who, after familiarizing himself with a previous version of this work, expressed his willingness to meet with me and spent three hours in discussion of the key ideas of the proposed theory. Furthermore, he persuaded me to eliminate a long metaphysical introduction and even wrote an "author's" Preface, which he suggested I use in place of my own. Preferring to give Sir Karl full credit for his own reflections, I have included his comments in the Post Script.

I also appreciate the help of R. Duncan Luce who thoroughly read a preceding version of the book and made numerous comments which contributed to a clearer description of some questions.

I have to thank Jack Adams-Webber, Alexander Borovik, Robert Garfias, Lev Levitin, Ernst McClain, Vladimir Rotar, Yuli Schreider, and Kirill Tyntarev for their valuable suggestions.

While working on the second edition, I have discussed many problems touched upon in it with William Baum, Lev Levitin, Jane O'Kelly, and Stefan Schmidt.

And as the first edition, the second edition became possible only thanks to invaluable help of my wife Victorina Lefebvre. This book is devoted to her.

PREFACE TO THE SECOND EDITION

In the first edition of this book, we have demonstrated that based on the intuitive ideas about human mental domain, it is possible to construct a model capable of explaining and predicting. In the first edition, we moved from unobservable mental phenomena to the acts of behavior that are possible to observe instrumentally. In the second edition, we include an additional chapter to describe another way of constructing the model: from behavior to the mental domain. It occurs that these two ways intersect. At their intersection, there is model of an organism capable of making choice. This model allows us to discover an unknown before connection between the entropy of input and that of the output of the system capable of making bipolar choice. This model also allowed us to suggest a new explanation for the Matching law formulated by Herrnstein and Baum concerning behavior of rats and pigeons in the experimental chamber.

INTRODUCTION TO THE FIRST EDITION

A psychological theory of bipolarity and reflexivity is sketched in this book. Bipolarity is not a new idea in psychology. Let us recall the basic works by Charles Osgood and George Kelly thanks to which bipolarity became an object of numerous experimental studies.

The special quality of our approach is that we begin not by analyzing experimental data but rather by constructing a theory based on a few axioms and obtain a theoretical model of the subject facing a choice between positive and negative poles. Our model is based on three axioms concisely expressing the sense of that which underlies the words 'free will' and one postulate concerning the linearity of the function corresponding to the subject with respect to each of its arguments.

It automatically follows from these assumptions that the subject possesses a special quality that we call reflexivity: he has an image of the self, which, in turn, also has an image of the self. At any given moment, the subject is in a particular state within a continuum of states. The theoretical analogue for the subject's activity is the projection of his state onto an external screen which is a set of objects. For example, the choice of an action is the projection of a state onto a set of possible decisions; the estimated measurement of a stimulus with the help of a linear scale is the projection of a state onto a set of segments, and generation of a musical interval is the projection of a state onto a set of musical tones. In this way various types of human activity fit into the same simple scheme.

Our model allows us to offer explanations and predictions of psychological phenomena traditionally related to different areas of psychology. For example, we demonstrate that the categorization of measurable stimuli obeys a rational law; we predict that the median of distribution of votes received by winning alternatives on referendums is equal to 62%; we offer an explanation for a certain type of altruistic behavior, and we deduce formally the Just Intonation set of musical intervals.

Such a broad spectrum of applications gives us a reason to suppose that the phenomenon of human consciousness is generated by a specialized functional processor and that our model reflects some of the formal principles of its work. These considerations can be useful not only for psychologists but also for specialists searching brain correlations for the processes of consciousness.

We cannot exclude the possibility that human consciousness obeys algebraic rules as fundamental as those for the physical world. We can even suppose that in the future, deep relations between the phenomenon of man and the phenomena of the physical world will be established precisely on an algebraic level. For this reason at the end of book, we extract an algebraic object from our model; this object is called gamma-algebra and constitutes the model's formal frame.

In the Conclusion the author formulates three conjectures which should allow us to test experimentally the theory proposed in this book.

PART I
A MODEL OF THE SUBJECT WITH FREE WILL

Free will is the nucleus of the *phenomenon of man*. This statement can be considered the result of millennia-long attempts by human beings to comprehend themselves. This is why we base our model on the three axioms which, in our opinion, reflect the core of the meaning people attribute to the words 'free will'. We are constructing a model of man together with his inner domain. In doing so we use such terms as *an image of the self, inner feelings, intensity of belief*, and others which sound ordinary only in the context of phenomenological or psychoanalytical studies. In this work, these terms take on a technical meaning. We try to relate them to the clear formal constructions rather than to the hazy shadows of introspection. For example, in answering the question "what is an image of the self?", we will be able to draw a formula representing the subject on the blackboard and indicate a fragment corresponding to the image of the self instead of engaging in lengthy self-analytical considerations.

1.1. An Abstract Scheme

We assume that the subject lives in a world in which there are two poles: *positive* and *negative*. The world consists of situations, and the subject faces a choice between these two poles in every situation. At the level of sensations and primitive desires, the world presses on the subject. Two numbers, x_1 and $1 - x_1$ ($0 \leq x_1 \leq 1$), correspond to this pressure: x_1 is a measure of the pressure toward the positive pole and $1 - x_1$ toward the negative pole. The subject has *an image of the world*, and two numbers, x_2 and $1 - x_2$ ($0 \leq x_2 \leq 1$), correspond to this image: x_2 is a measure of the world pressure toward the positive pole, from the subject's point of view (a measure of the positivity of the subject's image of the world); $1 - x_2$ is a measure of the world pressure toward the negative pole, from the subject's point of view (a measure of the negativity of the subject's image of the world). In every situation, the subject has *intentions* to choose poles: x_3 is the measure of the intention to choose the positive pole and $1 - x_3$ to choose the negative pole ($0 \leq x_3 \leq 1$). Each pair, X_1 and $1 - X_1$, corresponds to the subject's state of *readiness* to perform a choice: X_1 is the measure of the readiness to choose the positive pole, and $1 - X_1$ of the readiness to choose the negative pole ($0 \leq X_1 \leq 1$). If $X_1 = 1$, then the subject is *ready* to choose the positive pole; if $X_1 = 0$, then the subject is *ready* to choose the negative pole.

Note that we distinguish between the mere subjective intention to perform a choice and the subject's objective state of readiness to do so. The subject's theoretical analogue is operator *Sub* which maps the set of values x_3 onto the set of values X_1. This operator depends on x_1 and x_2. We will write its actions as follows:

$$Sub_{x_1,x_2}(x_3) = X_1. \tag{1.1.1}$$

We say that the intention transforms or turns into the readiness if

$$x_3 = X_1. \tag{1.1.2}$$

Formally, condition (1.1.2) means that the operator is applied to its fixed point.

1.2. Axioms

In introducing the axioms we will limit our consideration of free will to the framework of moral choice, in order to make the meaning of the axioms more clear. We assume, however, that these axioms are correct not only in the moral domain but also in others where the relation positive-negative is defined.

Before we start a more detailed discussion, let us make two notes. First, free will cannot be reduced to probabilistic uncertainty, because it assumes not only the freedom of choosing between concrete alternatives, but also the freedom to choose a probability of their appearance. We can interpret a pair x_3 and $1 - x_3$ as a distribution which the subject is planning to use, and a pair X_1 and $1 - X_1$ as a distribution characterizing the subject's actual choice.

Second, free will is not absolute. It cannot be exercised all the time. There are circumstances which force a human being to perform good or bad actions independently of the intentions.

In the language of our representation, a statement "the subject is free to choose any distribution of probabilities in choosing alternatives" means that there exists at least one pair of values $x_1 = a$ and $x_2 = b$ for which *Sub* is an *identity operator*:

$$Sub_{a,b}(X) = X \qquad (1.2.1)$$

for any $X \in [0,1]$, where $X = x_3 = X_1$.

In other words, for $x_1 = a$ and $x_2 = b$ any of the subject's intentions is transformed into readiness.

What does it mean that under certain circumstances a person's choice of good or bad actions is determined independently of the person's intentions? It means that there exist at least two pairs of values $x_1 = c$, $x_2 = d$ and $x_1 = e$ and $x_2 = f$ such that

$$Sub_{c,d}(x_3) = 1 \qquad (1.2.2)$$

and

$$Sub_{e,f}(x_3) = 0 \qquad (1.2.3)$$

for any $x_3 \in [0.1]$.

Let us introduce three axioms in accordance with equations (1.2.1), (1.2.2), and (1.2.3).

I. The Axiom of Free Will

For all $X \in [0,1]$, $Sub_{0,0}(X) = X$.

II. The Axiom of Non-Evil Intent

For all $x_2, x_3 \in [0,1]$, $Sub_{1,x_2}(x_3) = 1$.

III. The Axiom of Credulity

For all $x_3 \in [0,1]$, $Sub_{0,1}(x_3) = 0$.

The axiom of free will (I) states that, if the world pushes subject to perform a negative action ($x_1 = 0$), and if, in addition, the subject sees the world doing so ($x_2 = 0$), then any intention of the subject turns into readiness ($x_3 = X_1 = X$), that is, the subject's readiness to perform an action depends only on the subject's intentions. The meaning of this axiom may be clarified as follows. Philosophical tradition dating back to Augustine ties a person's free will to the responsibility for actions (see discussion of these problems in Losskii, 1927; Glover, 1970; Kenny, 1978). When we state that someone is free to perform or not to perform an action, we assume that this person is responsible for the action. And vice versa, if we state that someone is responsible for the action, we assume that this person was free while performing it. We may now reformulate Axiom I with the following terms: if the world pushes subject to perform a bad action ($x_1 = 0$) and the subject knows this ($x_2 = 0$), then the subject is responsible for the action if it is performed.

The axiom of non-evil intent (II) states that if the world pushes subject to perform a good action ($x_1 = 1$), the subject always does so ($X_1 = 1$); that is, the subject would never perform a bad action. In other words, a human being is not a source of evil.

The axiom of credulity (III) states that if the subject perceives the world to be ideal ($x_2 = 1$, that is, from the subject's point of view, the world never pushes subject to perform a bad action), then the subject is ready to transform into action any of the world's demands for a negative action (if $x_1 = 0$, then $X_1 = 0$). This is a subject who "knows not what he does."

1.3. Deduction of the Analytical Representation of the Subject

Operator (1.1.1) can be represented as follows:

$$X_1 = f(x_1, x_2, x_3) . \qquad (1.3.1)$$

Let function $f(x_1, x_2, x_3)$ be *linear* in relation to each argument $x_1, x_2,$ and x_3. Then the following theorem is true.

Theorem 1: It follows from axioms I, II, and III that

$$f(x_1, x_2, x_3) = x_1 + (1 - x_1 - x_2 + x_1 x_2) x_3. \quad (1.3.2)$$

Proof: (1) Since function $f(x_1, x_2, x_3)$ is linear in relation to each of the variables, x_1, x_2, and x_3, it can be presented in a three-linear form

$$f(x_1, x_2, x_3) = a_0 + a_1 x_1 + a_2 x_2 + a_3 x_3 + a_4 x_1 x_2 + a_5 x_1 x_3 + a_6 x_2 x_3 + a_7 x_1 x_2 x_3,$$

where a_i ($i = 0, \ldots, 7$) are real numbers.

(2) From Axiom I: $f(0,0,x_3) = x_3$, and so $a_0 = 0$ and $a_3 = 1$.

(3) From Axiom II: $f(1, x_2, x_3) = 1$, so $a_1 = 1$, $a_5 = -1$, $a_2 + a_4 = 0$, and $a_6 + a_7 = 0$.

(4) From Axiom III: $f(0,1,x_3) = 0$, so $a_2 = 0$, $a_4 = 0$, $a_6 = -1$, and $a_7 = 1$. ∎

Thus, equation (1.3.1) can be written as

$$X_1 = x_1 + (1 - x_1 - x_2 + x_1 x_2) x_3, \quad (1.3.3)$$

or equally

$$X_1 = 1 - (1 - x_3 + x_2 x_3) + x_1 (1 - x_3 + x_2 x_3). \quad (1.3.4)$$

Let us introduce an auxiliary function $F(v_1, v_2)$ with equation

$$F(v_1, v_2) = 1 - v_2 + v_1 v_2, \quad (1.3.5)$$

where v_1 and v_2 are real numbers. Now expression (1.3.4) can be represented as

$$X_1 = F(x_1, F(x_2, x_3)). \quad (1.3.6)$$

We can prove that representation of function X_1 in the form of expression (1.3.6) is unique.

Theorem 2: Function

$$F(v_1, v_2) = 1 - v_2 + v_1 v_2$$

is the unique solution of the equation

$$\Phi(x_1, \Phi(x_2, x_3)) = x_1 + (1 - x_1 - x_2 + x_1 x_2) x_3, \quad (i)$$

where x_1, x_2, x_3 take on any value from $[0,1]$ and all values of $\Phi(x_2, x_3)$ belong to the interval $[0,1]$.

Proof: Let $x_2 = 0$ and $x_3 = 0$ in equation (i). Then $\Phi(x_1,p) = x_1$, where $p = \Phi(0,0)$. In this way function $\Phi(v_1,v_2)$, where $v_1,v_2 \in [0, 1]$, can take on any value from the interval $[0,1]$.

Because the right-hand side of (i) is linear with respect to x_1,

$$\Phi(x_1,\Phi(x_2,x_3)) = a(\Phi(x_2,x_3)) + (1 - a(\Phi(x_2,x_3)))x_1 , \qquad (ii)$$

where $a(u)$ is a function and

$$a(\Phi(x_2,x_3)) = x_3 - x_2 x_3 . \qquad (iii)$$

It follows from equation (i) and the fact that function $\Phi(v_1,v_2)$ can take on any value from the interval $[0, 1]$ that $\Phi(1,v_2) = 1$; from this and from equation (iii), when $x_2 = 1$, it follows that

$$a(1) = 0. \qquad (iv)$$

By analogy to (ii) we represent $\Phi(x_2,x_3)$ as

$$\Phi(x_2,x_3) = a(x_3) + (1 - a(x_3))x_2 ,$$

or

$$\Phi(x_2,x_3) = a(x_3)(1 - x_2) + x_2 . \qquad (v)$$

Substituting (v) into (i) gives

$$\Phi(x_1, a(x_3)(1 - x_2) + x_2) = x_1 + (1 - x_1 - x_2 + x_1 x_2)x_3 , \qquad (vi)$$

from which for $x_3 = 1$ follows

$$\Phi(x_1,x_2) = 1 - x_2 + x_1 x_2 ,$$

and finally

$$\Phi(v_1,v_2) = 1 - v_2 + v_1 v_2 = F(v_1,v_2) \qquad \blacksquare$$

Let us suppose that the subject has an image of the self. We put this image into correspondence with the function

$$X_2 = F(x_2,x_3) . \qquad (1.3.7)$$

The value of X_2 can be interpreted as the subject's readiness to choose a positive pole, from the subject's point of view (a measure of the positivity of the image of the self). In this interpretation, the subject is represented by the same function $F(v_1, v_2)$ both from our point of view (1.3.6) and from his own (1.3.7); variable v_1 stands for the world's influence and variable v_2 for the image of the self. Variable x_3 acquires an additional sense: it represents the image of the self's image of the self.

We can simplify our notation of the function $F(v_1, v_2)$. Let the 'exponent' $v_1^{v_2}$ be understood not in the traditional sense but as a contraction of the expression on the right-hand side of equation (1.3.5):

$$v_1^{v_2} =_{def} 1 - v_2 + v_1 v_2, \qquad (1.3.8)$$

then (1.3.6) can be represented as

$$X_1 = x_1^{x_2^{x_3}}. \qquad (1.3.9)$$

Let us note that for the values $v_1, v_2 \in \{0, 1\}$ the following expressions are true: $1^1 = 1$, $1^0 = 1$, $0^1 = 0$, and $0^0 = 1$. Therefore, for these values of v_1 and v_2, function $v_1^{v_2}$ corresponds to the Boolean implication

$$v_2 \to v_1 = \overline{v_2} \vee v_1,$$

where Boolean variables v_1 and v_2 correspond to variables v_1 and v_2 in equation (1.3.8); the Boolean 1 corresponds to the arithmetical 1, and the Boolean 0 to the arithmetical 0. Thus, when x_1, x_2, x_3, and $X_1 \in \{0, 1\}$, equation (1.3.9) corresponds to the Boolean expression

$$X_1 = (x_3 \to x_2) \to x_1,$$

where Boolean variables x_1, x_2, x_3, and X_1 correspond to variables x_1, x_2, x_3, and X_1.

1.4. The Fixed Points of Operator *Sub*

Using equation (1.3.9) we can represent the operator as

$$Sub = x_1^{x_2^{[\,]}}, \qquad (1.4.1)$$

where [ ] is the place for variable x_3.

The fixed points of this operator are given by the equation

$$X = x_1^{x_2^{X}}, \qquad (1.4.2)$$

which is

$$X = x_1 + (1 - x_1 - x_2 + x_1 x_2)X. \qquad (1.4.3)$$

By solving equation (1.4.3), we find that for $x_1 + x_2 > 0$,

$$X = X_1 = x_3 = \frac{x_1}{x_1 + x_2 - x_1 x_2}, \qquad (1.4.4)$$

and for $x_1 + x_2 = 0$, i.e., when $x_1 = 0$ and $x_2 = 0$,

$$X = X_1 = x_3, \qquad (1.4.5)$$

where X being any number from the interval [0,1].

We will call the subject *intentional*, if for any pair x_1, x_2, his intention is a fixed point of operator *Sub*. In other words, the subject is intentional, if his readiness X_1 is equal to his intention x_3 for any $x_1, x_2 \in [0,1]$.

The following function corresponds to the subject's image of the self:

$$X_2 = F(x_2, x_3) = 1 - x_3 + x_2 x_3. \qquad (1.4.6)$$

Let us find now an expression for the intentional subject's image of the self. By substituting x_3 from (1.4.4) into (1.4.6), we find that for $x_1 + x_2 > 0$

$$X_2 = \frac{x_2}{x_1 + x_2 - x_1 x_2} \, . \qquad (1.4.7)$$

It follows from (1.4.5) and (1.4.6) that for $x_1 + x_2 = 0$

$$X_2 = 1 - X_1 \, , \qquad (1.4.8)$$

where X_1 any number from $[0,1]$.

PART II
GENERAL INTERPRETATION

2.1. Self-Reflexion, Trend, and Belief

We assume that the subject possesses certain qualities which we will call *trends*. There are two types of trends. In one, the subject's activity is focused on an external object, in the other - on the self. An external object is either the external world as a whole or any part of it.

Let us consider the graphic metaphor in Fig. 2.1.1, which corresponds to equation (1.3.9).

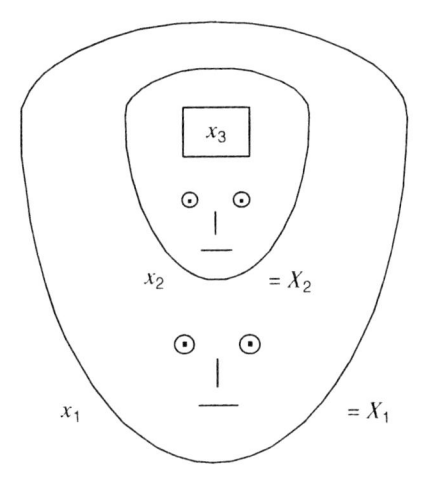

Fig. 2.1.1. A graphic metaphor.

The largest head corresponds to the subject; the head inserted into the first one is the subject's image of the self; the rectangle inside the second head corresponds to the model of the self. This model plays the role of the image of the self for the subject's image of the self. Such a structure of the subject is not postulated, but rather deduced from the assumptions given above.

Let the subject, in addition to an image of the self, have a model of the self. From a psychological point of view, an image of the self is a direct 'vision' of the self by the subject. It is *me* for the subject. The fact that this is a special representation of the self is not realized by the subject (see Lefebvre, 1992). A model of the self, in contrast to the image of the self, is realized by subject namely as a representation of the self. It is *my image of me* for the subject. A pronoun 'my' refers to 'the image of the self', thus *a model of the self* is "the image of the self's image of the self." We consider *a model of the self* as a specific subject who can be characterized by his readiness to choose a positive pole which is identical to the intention of the 'main' subject to choose a positive pole with measure x_3.

Let us introduce now the theoretical analogues for inner feelings. We assume that the more negative the subject's image of the world, the more intense the feeling of the world, and the more negative the subject's image of the self, the more intense the feeling of the self. The value

$$d = 1 - x_2 \qquad (2.1.1)$$

will be called the subject's *feeling of the world* and the value

$$D = 1 - X_2 \qquad (2.1.2)$$

the subject's *feeling of the self* (Lefebvre, 1984, 1987, 1990).

We assume also that the subject is able to 'feel' intentions. The intensity of such feelings is

$$s = 1 - x_3. \qquad (2.1.3)$$

Thus, the more negative the subject's intentions, the more intense his feelings of intention.

Let us now provide the subject with the ability to believe. Imagine that the subject has to answer a question: is the world good or bad? In this case, the value of x_2 is the measure of positivity of the subject's image of the world, and the value of x_3 is the measure of the subject's intention to say 'the world is good'. Respectively, $d = 1 - x_2$ is the measure of negativity of the subject's image of the world, and $s = 1 - x_3$

is the measure of the subject's intention to say 'the world is bad'. The relation between any two values d and s are represented as

$$d = rs, \qquad (2.1.4)$$

where r is a real number. Equality $r = 1$ means that the measure of the subject's intention to say 'the world is bad' is equal to the measure of the negativity of his image of the world; $r > 1$ means that the subject underestimates the degree of the negativity of his image of the world, and $r < 1$ means that he overestimates it.

In the framework of our model, the 'phenomenon of belief' in relation to the world is the subject's ability to deviate from evaluations imposed on him by his previous perceptive experience. This experience is presented in the model as the value of d.

The value of r shows by 'how many times' the subject under- or overestimates the degree of the world's negativity in his image of the world. We will use this value as the measure of the subject's belief: the greater the value of r, the stronger his belief in the positivity of the world.

Imagine now that the subject has to answer a question: is he good or bad? In this case, the value of X_2 is the measure of the positivity of his image of the self, and the value of x_3 is the measure of the subject's intention to say 'I am good.' Conversely, $D = 1 - X_2$ is the measure of the negativity of the subject's image of the self and $s = 1 - x_3$ is the measure of the subject's intention to say 'I am bad'. The relation between two values D and s are represented as

$$D = Rs, \qquad (2.1.5)$$

where R is a real number. Expression $R = 1$ means that the measure of the subject's intention to say 'I am bad' is equal to the measure of the negativity of his image of the self; $R > 1$ means that the subject underestimates the degree of the negativity of his image of the self, and $R < 1$ means that he overestimates it. We will consider the value of R as the measure of the subject's belief that he is good: the greater R, the stronger the subject's belief.

We will call r *an index of belief* for the world-trend and R *an index of belief* for the self-trend. We will consider that if $r < 1$ ($R < 1$), the belief to positivity is weak rather than strong, and if $r > 1$ ($R > 1$), the belief to positivity is strong rather than weak. The values $r = 1$ and $R = 1$ correspond to the point of balance between strong and weak belief.

2.2. Quantum-Mechanical Analogy

It has been suggested in the works of Chavchanidze (1967), Orlov (1981), and Oshins & McGoveran (1980) that human choice can be regarded as the reduction of a wave function. We will use this metaphor and consider the transition from the state of readiness to a choice of a concrete alternative as a reduction of function (1.3.9).

Suppose the subject can be in a continuum of various states, which are in a one-to-one correspondence with the values of variable X_1. Each state corresponds to the subject's readiness to choose a positive pole with measure X_1 and a negative pole with measure $1 - X_1$. We will call the states corresponding to $X_1 = 1$ and $X_1 = 0$, *pure*, and all the others *mixed*. The subject's transition from a mixed state to a pure one will be called *reduction*. We assume that the value of X_1 characterizing a mixed state is a *conditional probability* of its transition to a positive state, if the reduction takes place.

Let us now introduce the analogue of a measuring device. We will call it a *screen*. The screen is a set of elements which we call *rulers*. Let us put this set into a one-to-one correspondence with a set of different non-negative numbers $\{e\}$, which has a maximal number e_{max} and a minimal number 0. The ruler which corresponds to e_{max} will be called *unit*, and the one corresponding to 0 - *zero-ruler*. We will refer to the value e/e_{max} as the size of the ruler corresponding to number e.

We will consider two types of *screens*. A screen of the first type consists of two rulers: the unit and the zero-ruler. A screen of the second type consists of the continuum of rulers corresponding to all non-negative numbers e for which the inequality $e \leq e_{max}$ holds.

The analogue of a measurement procedure is the subject's *contact* to the screen. As a result of this contact the subject's state is projected onto the screen. Establishing a one-to-one correspondence between the subject's state (after a contact with the screen) and a ruler of size X_1 characterizing the subject's state will be called *projecting* the subject's state onto the screen. The ruler itself will be called the *projection*.

Only pure states are projected onto a screen of the first type. If such a screen contacts a subject who is in a mixed state, then the contact causes reduction, after which a pure state is projected onto the screen. If a screen of the second type contacts a subject who is in a mixed state, the reduction does not take place, and the mixed state is projected onto the screen.

It is worth noting the difference between this schema and quantum mechanics. In the latter, measurement of the mixed state is always connected with reduction. In our schema, it is possible to measure an uncertain state without reduction.

2.3. Projecting the State onto a Screen as the Object's Reference

What is the purpose of projecting the subject onto a screen? It consists in establishing the *relation of reference* between the object and the screen. For example, when a controller evaluates the quality of a manufactured article with the help of a ten-mark scale, he establishes a relation between a real object, on which his activity is focused, and a screen. The screen in this case is a set of ten segments beginning with point 1 and ending with points 1, 2, ..., 10 respectively. The segment [1,1] plays the role of a zero-ruler, the segment [1,10] that of a unit. In the framework of these relationships, a mark on the scale acquires a status of 'graphic judgment' about the object.

The relation of reference appears, when the subject evaluates his own driving skills with the help of a scale. In this case we are concerned with relationships between the screen and the subject himself.

There is also a case, when the object on which the subject's activity is focused is the screen itself. Then the screen with a mark on it is both the object and the graphical judgment about itself. Such a relationship will be called *the self-reference of the screen*. We connect a screen's self-reference with the generation of ideal proportions in graphic art and music.

The main idea can be clarified as follows. Let the subject in state X_1 be an artist who is searching for a point on a segment which would divide this segment into an aesthetically attractive ratio. We can consider this segment the object on which the subject's activity is focused. Suppose now that this segment, independently of the artist's cognizant activity, performs the function of a screen to which the artist's state is projected. Let the length of the segment be equal to 1. At the moment when the artist's pencil, which is moving along the segment, appears at the distance X_1 from one of its ends, a mixed state is projected, the pencil stops, and the artist realizes this stop as the choice of the proportion sought.

Consider now the generation of musical intervals. A musical interval is a psychoacoustical phenomenon related to the generation and perception of two musical tones sounding simultaneously or consecutively. A musical interval has a particular size. Its size is either the ratio of the frequencies of tones constituting the interval or the ratio of the strings' lengths corresponding to these tones (which is the reverse of the ratio of frequencies).

Let us choose a tone and call it a unit. We designate the length of an ideal string which corresponds to this tone e_{max}. Consider the set of all tones which are of higher pitch than the chosen one. The lengths of the ideal strings corresponding to these tones satisfy the inequality $e < e_{max}$. We can consider the set of these tones, together with the tone-unit, a screen. The generation of a sounding interval which corresponds to ratio e/e_{max} can be considered as creating the screen and projecting the subject's state onto it: the lower tone defines the screen, and the higher tone is a projection of the subject's state onto this screen.

A geometrical screen and a musical screen differ essentially from one another. The segment along which the artist is moving the pencil is an external object in relation to the artist, since the segment exists independently from the artist's activity.

A lower tone which defines the screen does not have its own existence independent of the musician. Both its generation and the short time of its existence depend on the musician's activity. (For example, a violinist must move a bow to keep the tone sounding.) This is the reason why we cannot regard a musical tone as an external object in relation to a musician. Therefore, we presume that during the generation of a geometrical proportion the subject's activity is focused on an external object, and that during the generation of musical intervals the subject's activity is focused on himself. Parts VII and VIII analyze this problem in detail.

PART III

DECISIONS BASED ON THE IMAGE OF THE WORLD

3.1. Application of the Model to the Empirical Domain

We will consider the intentional subject (see section 1.4), that is, from a formal point of view, we will search for the fixed point of operator *Sub*. To apply our model empirically we must do the following:

1. Find the object on which the subject's activity is focused.
2. Find what entity serves as a screen in a given situation.
3. Establish the values of x_1 and x_2.
4. Write an equation and analyze it.

We would like to emphasize once more that we will use the model both inside and outside the framework of the moral domain. The dichotomy moral-immoral is only a particular case of a more general positive-negative dichotomy.

3.2. Categorization of Stimuli

In this section we will demonstrate a new approach to an old psychophysical problem. The essence of the problem is that the results of estimating measurable properties of stimuli (such as length, weigh, duration, etc.) differ according to which of two methods is used (Helson, 1947; Parducci, 1956; Stevens & Galanter, 1957).

The first method is called *magnitude estimation*. The subject is assigned the task of estimating a magnitude with the help of a unit of measurement, for example, the length of a line in inches, or the weight of a load in ounces. Figure 3.2.1 shows a graph for the magnitude estimation of the length of seventeen steel bars evenly distributed in length between 4 cm and 111 cm (constructed on experimental data from Stevens & Galanter, 1957). The horizontal axis corresponds to a physical scale, and vertical axis to a magnitude scale.

The second method is called *categorization*, that is, an assignment of each stimulus to one of a set of categories corresponding to levels of intensity. One of the widespread methods of categorization is as follows. First the subject is presented with stimuli of a maximum and minimum magnitudes. Then the subject is asked to estimate the magnitude of each stimulus with reference to a scale divided into k labels (1 corresponds to the stimulus with the least magnitude, and k to the one with the greatest). Figure 3.2.1 also shows a graph of categorization for the same steel bars with reference to a scale having 11 labels.

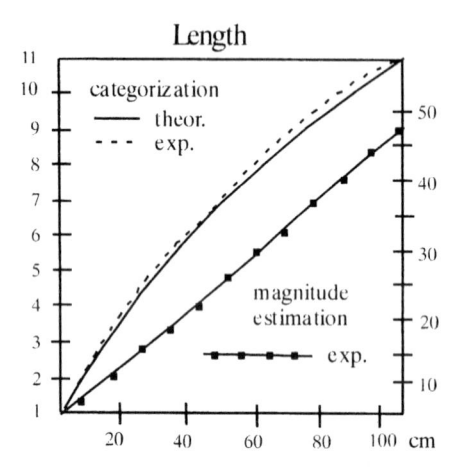

Fig. 3.2.1. Graphs of Categorization and Magnitude Estimation.

The right vertical line corresponds to the magnitude scale, and the left one to the categorical scale. The theoretical curve is produced with equation (3.2.4)

We can see that the curves resulting from the magnitude and categorical estimations are different. While magnitude estimation produces an almost straight line, the graph of categorical estimation is a convex curve which is symmetrical relative to the diagonal of the square. Curves of this shape are produced not only for length but for other modalities as well (see Fig.3.2.2 and Fig.3.2.3 constructed on experimental data from Stevens & Galanter, 1957).

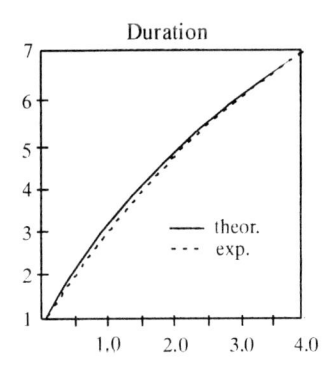

Fig. 3.2.2. A Graph of Categorization

Categorization (on a 7-point scale) of the duration of 16 time intervals equally distributed between 0.25 sec. and 4 sec. and presented equal number of times. The theoretical curve is produced by equation (3.2.4).

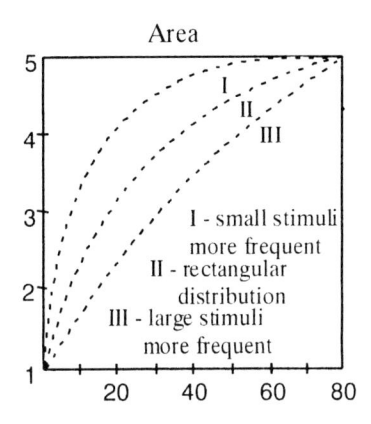

Fig. 3.2.3. A Graph of Categorization

Categorization of the areas of 9 rectangles on a 5-point scale.

There were many attempts to explain the mechanism of this curvature (Stevens & Galanter, 1957; Anderson, 1981; Marks, 1968; Birnbaum, 1982; Krueger, 1989), but no theoretical model has been constructed.

Another phenomenon found in such experiments is that if weak stimuli are presented more often than the strong ones, then convexity increases, and if strong stimuli are presented more often than weak ones, convexity decreases in comparison with the results obtained by presenting strong and weak stimuli an equal number of times (Stevens & Galanter, 1957; Parducci, 1956) (see Fig.3.2.3).

The best-known explanation of it is the Range-Frequency model by Parducci (1965). One of the main postulates underlying this theory (which contains a free parameter) states that the subjects have the tendency to equalize the frequencies of the different categories used. Let us note that this tendency follows from our theory. Therefore, Parducci's model can be partially reduced to the formal model of the subject developed in this work.

Suppose that the maximal and the minimal stimuli are the only ones presented as 'special'. None of the others is to be distinguished by the frequency of its presentation or in any other way. Without this assumption the categorical scale might acquire, aside from its termini, other special points which could turn it into a composite of several scales.

Let us compare this experiment with our model.

1. In each interaction, the subject's activity is focused on an external stimulus (for example, a metal stick).

2. The role of the screen is played by a categorical scale, which can be considered a continuous interval [0,1], where number 0 corresponds to category 1, and number 1 to category k.

3. Variable x_1 corresponds to the psychological impression produced by a concrete stimulus. Variable x_2 corresponds to the averaged psychological impression of stimuli preceding a given stimulus.

4. The subject corresponds to the equation:

$$X = \frac{x_1}{x_1 + x_2 - x_1 x_2}.$$

Let us analyze this correspondence in detail. We assume that there is a continuous function $\psi = G(g)$, where g is the value of the physical magnitude of a certain stimulus: $g \in [g_{min}, g_{max}]$, and ψ is the value of the psychological impression from physical magnitude: $\psi \in [\psi_{min}, \psi_{max}]$. The value of ψ monotonically increases when g increases. The categorical scale consists of k equidistant marks on a segment, two of which coincide with its ends. For the sake of convenience let us consider ψ_{min} as corresponding to mark 1, and ψ_{max} as corresponding to mark k.

The value of variable X corresponds to the normalized value $\hat{Q}$ categorical estimation expressed in the length of the categorical scale:

$$\hat{Q} = \frac{Q-1}{k-1}, \qquad (3.2.1)$$

where Q is the value for categorical estimation on a scale from 1 to k. The value of variable x_1 corresponds to the normalized psychological impression $\hat{\psi}$:

$$\hat{\psi} = \frac{\psi - \psi_{min}}{\psi_{max} - \psi_{min}}, \qquad (3.2.2)$$

where ψ is the psychological impression produced by a given stimulus (Parducci, 1965). For such magnitudes as length and duration, psychological impression and a stimulus' physical value are connected linearly.

The value of variable x_2 corresponds to the mean value of normalized psychological impressions from stimuli preceding a given one. For long series, which are constructed in such a way that the mean value computed on the base of the first few presentations does not change much with following presentations, we can presume that x_2, corresponds to the mean value of normalized psychological impressions from the stimuli of the whole series.

We can consider the process of categorization as the projection of a mixed state onto a scale. But in a long series of stimuli mentioned above, each series corresponds to a constant value x_2. Let us now 'read' expression (3.2.3) as the equation of a family of rational functions given by parameter x_2 (Fig.3.2.4):

$$X = \frac{x_1}{x_1 + x_2 - x_1 x_2}.\qquad(3.2.3)$$

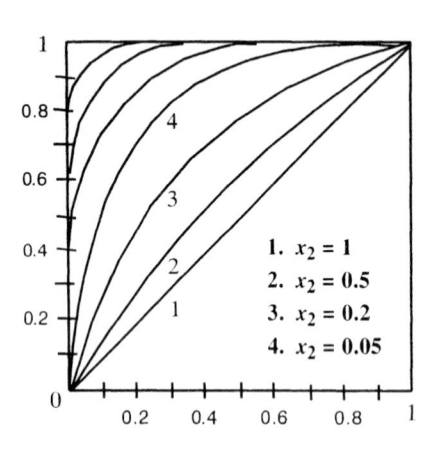

1. $x_2 = 1$
2. $x_2 = 0.5$
3. $x_2 = 0.2$
4. $x_2 = 0.05$

Fig. 3.2.4. A family of rational functions given by equation (3.2.3).

This family models the experimental data: graphs are symmetrical in relation to a square diagonal and they become more convex with the decrease of x_2, which corresponds to the phenomena found in experiments (Fig.3.2.3). If the frequencies of presentation of different equidistant stimuli are equal to each other, then $x_2 = 1/2$, from which

$$X = \frac{2x_1}{1 + x_1}.\qquad(3.2.4)$$

A graph of the corresponding curve is given on Figs.3.2.1 and 3.2.2. We see that it is close to the experimental curves.

Therefore, we have grounds to assume that we have deduced a new *rational law* for the categorization of stimuli with measurable properties.

3.3. Estimation of Stars' Brightness

A categorical estimation of the intensity of stimuli is one of the oldest known psychological methods. In the second century B.C., Greek astronomer Hipparchus introduced a quantitative scale for estimating the brightness of the stars. He assigned the first category to the stars that appear the brightest, and the sixth to the weakest, barely visible ones. To the rest of the stars, depending on their brightness, intermediate categories were assigned. This scale had been used by astronomers for more than two thousand years until objective photometric methods were invented in the nineteenth century. Fig.3.3.1 shows a graph correlating photometric and subjective estimations of stars' brightness.

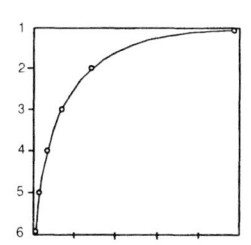

Fig. 3.3.1. Correlation between visual evaluations of star brightness and their photometric objective intensity.

A vertical axis corresponds to the categorical estimations, and horizontal axis to the photometric ones (the graph is made based on Jastrow's (1887) data).

Since the curve in Fig.3.3.1 resembles a logarithmic curve, it has been suggested that the human eye evaluates brightness on a logarithmic scale (for a background see Stevens, 1975). This assumption had quickly won broad support that had lasted until Stevens (1936) brought weighty statements against the logarithmic law. While analyzing this phenomenon, Stevens realized that the graph in Fig.3.3.1 resembles the logarithmic one, only because there are many more dim stars than bright ones in the sky. Underlying this assumption was the discovery that a magnitude scale for the estimation of the brightness of point sources briefly flashed (what stars are) is connected linearly with a photometric scale. This allowed Stevens to consider the horizontal axis in Fig.3.3.1 to be a magnitude scale. The distribution of stimuli for astronomers is shifted toward the weak ones, and therefore, the experimental graph is as convex as a logarithmic one. To verify this hypothesis, Stevens created an 'experimental sky' where 'stars' were evenly distributed and came to a conclusion that the categorical curve was not logarithmic (Stevens, 1975).

In accordance with the above considerations, we can assume that the curve in Fig.3.3.1 is a *rational function*, whose convexity depends on the value of x_2. Since the number of the dim stars is significantly higher, the value of x_2 is small, and the curve is very convex. In Stevens' experiment, x_2 was close to 0.5 and, thus, the curve was less convex (see Fig.3.2.4).

3.4. Altruism

Thousands of years of observation of human nature have resulted in the judgment that people who commit a wrong and feel remorse become more inclined toward altruism. In our time this observation seems to be supported by experimental data (Berscheid & Walster, 1967; Brock & Becker, 1966; Darlington & Macker, 1966; Freedman, Wallington, & Bless, 1967; Wallace & Sadalla, 1966; Carlsmith & Gross, 1969; see also Carlson & Miller, 1987). Moreover, a surprising fact has been found. It has been noticed that altruism increases not only when a person commits a wrong, but also when he is a witness to the 'injustice of the world' (Lerner, 1965; Lerner & Matthews, 1967; Simmons & Lerner, 1968). Regan (1971) conducted the following experiment. Students-subjects were hired ostensibly to conduct experiments with albino rats. Each subject had to apply a very weak electric shock to a rat. But the experimenter (unknown to the subjects) increased the power to make the rat jump suddenly and then declared that the experiment had failed. Some of the subjects were blamed for the failure of the experiment, while others were told that a short circuit had caused the power surge. Then the subjects were involved in a situation in which they were asked to donate a small amount of money to a summer student research project (which had no relation to their experiment). There was no difference between the two groups of subjects in their willingness to donate some money. In the control group, however, in which the subjects conducted the same experiments with the albino rats but without negative interruptions, the willingness to donate money was lower.

Let us analyze this experiment from the point of view of our schema.

1. The object of the subject's altruistic activity is a summer student research project.
2. The role of screen is performed by the alternative: do not donate - donate, in which 'donate' is the positive pole, and 'do not donate' is the negative pole.
3. Variable x_1 can take on any values except $x_1 = 1$, and variable x_2 is defined by the degree of positivity of the world observed by the subject ($x_2 > 0$).
4. The subject corresponds to equation

$$X = \frac{x_1}{x + x_2(1 - x_1)} . \tag{3.4.1}$$

It follows from (3.4.1) that X monotonically increases when x_2 decreases.

Suppose that before a rat jump from the electric shock, the subject is characterized by the value $x_2 = u_1$. After the shock, the subject's picture of the world changes. A new value appears: $x_2 = u_2$, and the world becomes less positive. Therefore, $u_2 < u_1$. It follows from (3.4.1) that

$$X(u_2) > X(u_1) . \tag{3.4.2}$$

Thus, after the rats receive the electric shock, the subject must become more altruistic than before, regardless of whether he feels responsible or not.

PART IV
THE AUTONOMOUS SUBJECT

In the previous chapter, we considered examples in which the subject's state was predetermined by the direct perceptive contact between the subject and the object on which the subject's activity is focused. In this chapter, we will extend the model to the case in which there is no such contact.

Let us require the subject to estimate the probability of the existence of intelligent life in the Andromeda nebula. The subject does not have the ability to sense the existence of life in the Andromeda nebula in the same way he can feel the presence of flowers in a dark room by their scent. Therefore, we cannot correlate the Andromeda nebula with a specific value of x_1.

The subject does not have any experience in the perception of life in other galaxies either, so, he does not have a generalized sensory picture of the galaxies in which intelligent life exists. There are no grounds, therefore, to ascribe any specific value to x_2

The subject will be called *autonomous* if his relation to the object on which his activity is focused is such that his decision cannot be grounded on perceptual information from this object or perceptual information obtained from similar objects in the past.

4.1. Four Assumptions on the Autonomous Subject

First. The autonomous subject is intentional, that is, X_1 is the fixed point of operator *Sub*.

Second. For the autonomous subject

$$x_1 = \frac{1}{2}, \qquad (4.1.1)$$

that is, the preference for one pole over the other is not innate in the subject.

Third. The autonomous subject's readiness to choose the positive pole depends on his trend and the index of belief.

Fourth. The values of the indexes of belief, R and r, are either positive integers or numbers inverse to them:

$$R = \begin{cases} k \\ 1, \\ \frac{1}{k} \end{cases} \quad r = \begin{cases} k \\ 1, \\ \frac{1}{k} \end{cases} \qquad (4.1.2)$$

where $k = 1, 2, \ldots$.

4.2. A Trend to the Self

Let us find function that connects X_1 with k, when $0 < x_1, x_2 < 1$. The following equations correspond to the intentional subject and his image of the self:

$$X_1 = \frac{x_1}{x_1 + x_2 - x_1 x_2}, \qquad (4.2.1)$$

$$X_2 = \frac{x_2}{x_1 + x_2 - x_1 x_2}. \qquad (4.2.2)$$

The feeling of one's negativity, D, and that of one's intention, s, are

$$D = 1 - X_2 = \frac{(1 - x_2)x_1}{x_1 + x_2 - x_1 x_2}, \qquad (4.2.3)$$

$$s = 1 - X_1 = \frac{(1 - x_1)x_2}{x_1 + x_2 - x_1 x_2}. \qquad (4.2.4)$$

In accordance with definition of R (see 2.1.5),

$$R = \frac{D}{s} = \frac{(1-x_2)x_1}{(1-x_1)x_2}. \tag{4.2.5}$$

When $x_1 = \frac{1}{2}$,

$$X_1 = \frac{1}{1+x_2}, \tag{4.2.6}$$

and

$$R = \frac{1-x_2}{x_2}, \tag{4.2.7}$$

hence,

$$x_2 = \frac{1}{R+1}. \tag{4.2.8}$$

By substituting x_2 from (4.2.8) to (4.2.6), we obtain

$$X_1 = \frac{R+1}{R+2}, \tag{4.2.9}$$

where R is either k or $1/k$, $k = 1, 2, \dots$.

The value of the readiness given by (4.2.9) corresponds to the *permissible* states of the autonomous subject with the trend to the self.

4.3. A Trend to an External Object

It follows from (4.2.6) that for $x_1 = \frac{1}{2}$,

$$x_2 = \frac{1-X_1}{X_1}. \tag{4.3.1}$$

The feeling of the world's negativity, d, and that of intention, s, are

$$\begin{aligned} d &= 1 - x_2 = \frac{2X_1 - 1}{X_1}, \\ s &= 1 - X_1. \end{aligned} \tag{4.3.2}$$

In accordance with definition (see 2.1.4),

$$r = \frac{d}{s} = \frac{2X_1 - 1}{X_1(1 - X_1)}. \tag{4.3.3}$$

The above equation can be rewritten as follows:

$$X_1^2 + \frac{2-r}{r}X_1 - \frac{1}{r} = 0, \tag{4.3.4}$$

and its positive root is

$$X_1 = \frac{r - 2 + \sqrt{4 + r^2}}{2r}, \tag{4.3.5}$$

r being either k or $1/k$, $k = 1, 2, \ldots$.

Table 4.3.1
Permissible values of X for an autonomous subject directed toward the world ($k \leq 5$)

k	$r = k$	approximation	$r = 1/k$	approximation
1	$\frac{\sqrt{5}-1}{2}$	0.618	$\frac{\sqrt{5}-1}{2}$	0.618
2	$\frac{\sqrt{2}}{2}$	0.707	$\frac{\sqrt{17}-3}{2}$	0.562
3	$\frac{\sqrt{13}-1}{6}$	0.768	$\frac{\sqrt{37}-5}{2}$	0.541
4	$\frac{\sqrt{5}+1}{4}$	0.809	$\frac{\sqrt{65}-7}{2}$	0.531
5	$\frac{\sqrt{29}+3}{10}$	0.839	$\frac{\sqrt{101}-9}{2}$	0.525

If $r \to \infty$, then $X \to 1$ monotonically. If $r \to 0$, then $X \to 1/2$ monotonically. In other words, the stronger the subject's belief in the positivity of the world, the greater his readiness to choose the positive pole. When r is close to zero, belief is weak, and his readiness to choose either pole is close to 1/2. To obtain continuous extension of function (4.3.5), we supplement the set of r with two more values: $r = \infty$, for which $X_1 = 1$, and $r = 0$, for which $X_1 = \frac{1}{2}$. Equation (4.3.5) shows the permissible values of the readiness to choose a positive pole for the autonomous subject with the trend to the world. Table 4.3.1 gives the permissible values of X_1 for $k \leq 5$. The problem of empirical verification of those values is discussed at the end of section 8.8.

Let us note that for $k = 1$, the value of X_1 is equal to the golden section:

$$X_1 = \frac{\sqrt{5}-1}{2} = 0.618... \quad . \tag{4.3.6}$$

PART V
DECISIONS BASED ON BELIEF

5.1. Pole of Belief, Index of Belief, and Projection of the Subject's State

In this chapter we will demonstrate the use of the model of the autonomous subject. To make this approach clear, let us continue with the example which opens the previous part. The subject is to choose a point on the following scale:

```
A •-------------------------------------------• B
There is no intelligent life      There is intelligent life
in the Andromeda nebula           in the Andromeda nebula
```

One of the ends of this scale plays the role of the pole of belief for the subject. (A question of which end takes upon itself this role lies outside the framework of this model.) We have assumed earlier that the subject's state is predetermined by the index of belief, r. Therefore, the projection of the subject's state onto a screen is given by the pair (α, r), where α is the pole of belief.

Let the subject choose a point on the following scale:

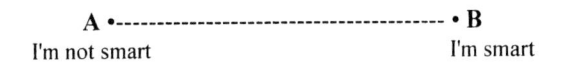

```
A •---------------------------------• B
I'm not smart                    I'm smart
```

The property of 'smartness' does not have such perceptive indications as length or weight, so that the subject cannot be said to 'perceive' the quality of his own mind. Thus we assume that his choice is based on belief. In this case the subject's activity is focused on the self, so his state projection onto the screen is given by the pair (α, R).

5.2. Social Choice

We will now demonstrate how the ideas developed in Part IV lead to understanding of a hitherto unknown phenomenon. As an example, consider a referendum being held on the following proposition:

> To decrease the number of optional subjects in public schools. This measure would both enable us to teach mandatory subjects better and would help balance the state budget.
>
> YES   NO

Let us introduce the following assumptions:

1. An ordinary voter does not have clear and particular information about the educational system, so his decision is based on belief rather than on an image of the world.

2. For the majority of voters, the semantic and syntactic formulation of the proposition (which constitutes its frame; see Tversky & Kahneman, 1981) predetermines the pole of belief and the shift of the r-value to the left or to the right of its balance point $r = 1$.

Suppose that in a given case the pole of belief is YES and $r \geq 1$. Under this assumption, the ordinary voter is described by the pair (α = YES, $r \geq 1$). The screen is a bipolar construct YES - NO. Thus, every choice the subject makes is a reduction of a mixed state. Because of the monotone dependence of X on r (see 4.3.5), the readiness of an ordinary voter to say YES is equal to or greater than the golden section value. Therefore, the percentage of votes for the winning pole is equal to or greater than 61.8%.

Let us now consider a set of free referenda and suppose that the formulation of each proposition predetermines the pole of belief and the shift of the r-value to the right or to the left of the balance point $r = 1$. Let us suppose also that for the entire set of propositions the probability of $r > 1$ is equal to the probability of $r < 1$. These assumptions lead us to a prediction which can be verified: the value 61.8% must be the *median* of vote distribution for winning poles. (Let us emphasize that the winning pole is the one which collected more than 50% of votes; it can be either YES or NO.) In other words, the number of propositions in which the winning pole collected more than 61.8% of votes must be equal to the number of propositions in which the winning pole collected less than 61.8% of votes.

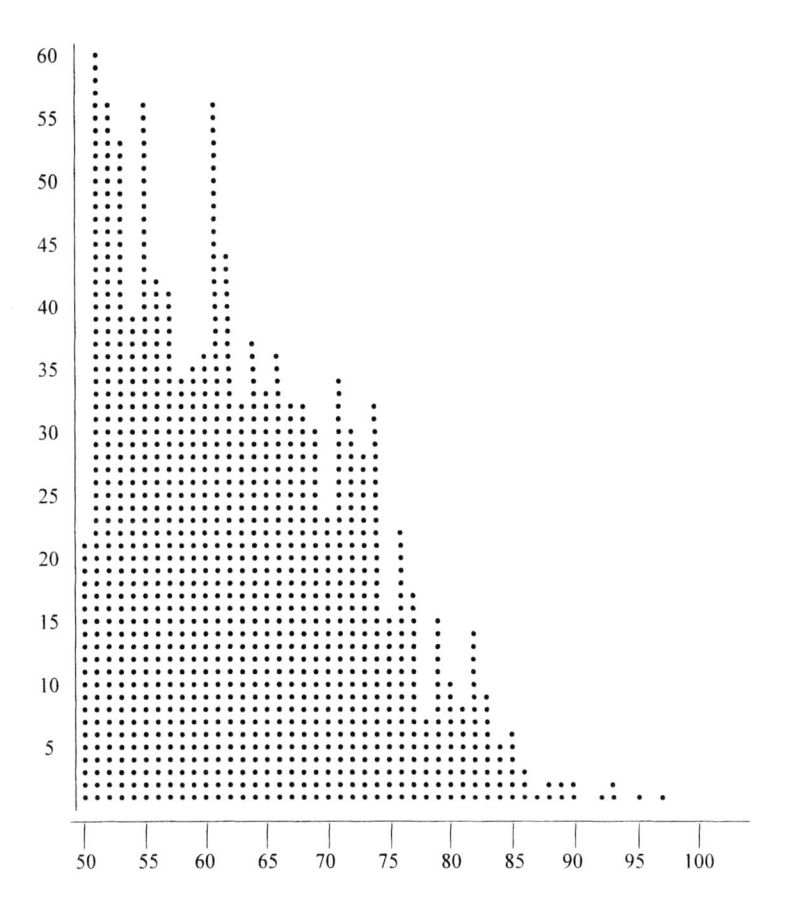

Fig.5.2.1. Graphs of California referenda from 1884-1990.

The horizontal axis represents percentages (from 50% to 100%); each dot corresponds to one proposition; a column of dots at each percent mark corresponds to all the propositions in which the winning pole collected the given percent of votes.

We have analyzed all the California referenda from 1884 through 1990 (Eu, 1983a,b; 1985a,b; 1987; 1989a,b,c). The distributions of the votes for the winning poles are shown on Fig.5.2.1.

The median of this distribution is equal to 62%. We can see also a local maximum in the area of the golden section value which may correspond to the cases with $r = 1$ (since the form of theoretical distribution is unknown, statistical evaluation of the significance of the peak at the golden section is extremely difficult).

A similar analysis has been done for referenda in Switzerland for the period from 1886 through 1978 (based on data from Butler & Ranney, 1978); the median of distribution is equal to 63%.

In addition we analyzed the data of referenda in Oregon for 1904-1914 (Barnett, 1915). The median is equal to 62%. Finally, we used all the samples of Ranney on referenda in America for 1978-1988 (Ranney, 1978, 1981, 1983, 1985, 1987, 1989). The median is 62%. We cannot rule out the possibility that the phenomenon of the median being equal to 62% demonstrates that it is a simplification to think that a referendum expresses a population's free choice on the essence of a problem. In reality the choice is predetermined in a great extent by the formulation of the question.

5.3 Categorization in the Bipolar Construct Good-Bad

Victorina D. Lefebvre (1990) conducted an experiment concerning the categorization of small objects according to the construct 'good - bad'. The objects to be categorized were 50 very similar pairs of beans sealed in small transparent envelopes (in order to eliminate tactile sensations). The subjects were asked to take the envelopes one by one, evaluate the beans as 'good' or 'bad', and put each envelope into the corresponding box. If the subject asked about criteria for evaluation, the experimenter suggested relying on intuition. There were 98 subjects, and the frequency of positive evaluations was 0.61.

We can explain this result as follows. Since there were no operational criteria for the objective measurement of the beans' good quality, the subjects made their decision based on belief. We can assume that beans as a class of things attract positive evaluations. Thus, the pole of belief is 'beans are good'. The average subject can be represented by the pair ($\alpha = a$ bean is good, $r = 1$), which explains why the frequency of positive choices in this experiment is close to the golden section value. The screen in this experiment is the bipolar construct 'good-bad', so that each choice is connected with the reduction of a mixed state.

5.4. The Golden Section and Choice of a Point on a Scale

In a study of moral judgments McGraw (1985) conducted the following experiment. Each subject was given a scenario of a particular action. It was a good action (a person returned a wallet he had found or helped a blind girl to collect money she had dropped) or a bad action (did not return the wallet, did not help the blind girl). The subject's task was to estimate the percentage of students who would behave according to the scenario. The subjects used a scale from 0% to 100% with increments of 10%. The subjects who were given a scenario with a good action indicated, on the average, that 62% of the students would behave this way; the subjects given a scenario with a bad action indicated, on the average, that 39% of the students would behave that way.

Thus, the numbers are close to the golden section value. We can explain these results by assuming that the pole of belief corresponds to the statement, "all the students perform good actions," and the index of belief $r = 1$. The screen in this case is a scale with percentages and not a binary construct, so reduction does not take place and the subject's mixed state, corresponding to $r = 1$, is projected onto the scale.

In the experimental study by Poulton, Simmonds, & Warren (1968) the subjects were shown a piece of gray paper (with a reflectance of 44%) on a white background (with a reflectance of 83%) and asked to indicate the 'lightness' of the paper expressed as a percentage considering white background to be 100% light.

Only the subject's very first judgment was registered (on a 0-100 scale). Fig.5.4.1 shows the data obtained by Poulton *et al.*

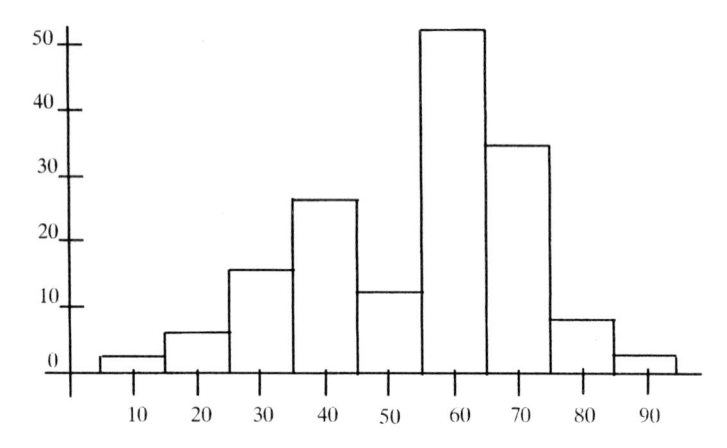

Fig. 5.4.1. The histogram of distribution of the dots in marking a 100-*mm* line for the very first time.

> The students avoid marking the line at the middle. The bias affects only the very first judgment (based on data from Poulton, 1989, p.168. Fig.78). Similar graphs (with a hollow in the middle) were obtained in the experiments on evaluation of the gray sample in comparison with white and black ones (the very first mark). See Poulton & Simmonds, 1985.

The shape of the curve is surprising: clearly the subjects avoided marking the middle of the line. The distribution on Fig.5.4.1 has peaks at points 60 and 40. Despite the insufficiency of the data, we would suggest that these peaks correspond to the golden section (60 looking from the left-hand edge, and 60 from the right). Making this assumption, we can explain the two-hump distribution with our model. In this experiment, when the subject makes his very first choice he does not have other samples of grey to enable him to construct a subjective scale of lightness or darkness. As a result, his sensation of lightness or darkness has no numerical measure. Thus, a grey sample on a light background cannot predetermine the value of x_1. Neither has the subject had any previous contacts with similar samples. So the value of x_2 is also undetermined. Therefore, we can consider the subject autonomous and his choice a projection of his state onto a screen, which in this case is the 0-100 segment. For some subjects, the pole of belief is point 100; that is, for them a sample belongs to a class of light objects. For others, the pole of belief is point 0; that is, for them a sample belongs to a class of dark objects. (Note that the concept of the pole of belief in the context of this experiment is kindred to the concept of a perceptive hypothesis). If we let $r = 1$, then we can predict the very results found in the experiment described above.

Similar curve shapes were obtained in the experiment by Poulton & Simmonds (1985), in which a grey sample was presented between black and white ones. In this case, the subjects' avoidance of the middle point can be also explained by an assumption that no scales for lightness or darkness are formed in the subject. As a result, variables x_1 and x_2 are not connected with perception; therefore, the subject's state is predetermined by the index of belief $r = 1$. We consider that this experiment can be used as a control for verification of our model (see Conclusion, *Conjecture 2*).

5.5. The Golden Section and 'Mere Exposure'

Apparently, the effect called 'mere exposure' (Zajonc, 1968; Harrison, 1977) is also related to the subject's projecting his inner state onto a screen. The essence of this phenomenon is that when subjects do not have objective criteria, they evaluate more positive the objects they know better. In one of the experiments (Zajonc, 1968), ten Chinese-like characters were first shown one by one to several groups of subjects who did not know the Chinese language. The characters were shown with five different levels of frequency, some only once, some twice, some five times, some ten times, and some 25 times. In the second phase of the experiment, the same characters (plus two new ones) were presented with equal frequency to the same subjects. They were told that all of the characters stood for adjectives and that the task was to guess the degree of positivity for each adjective and indicate it on a scale 0-6 (0 standing for 'bad' and 6 for 'good'). In analyzing Zajonc's data, we find that the mean value assigned by the subjects for the characters which were exposed most often (25 times) in the first phase of the experiment was 3.8. The value of this evaluation as a fraction of the scale length is (3.8)/6 ≈ 0.63. We can assume that in this experiment, the preliminary exposure of the characters predetermines the pole of belief. The subject 'believes' (with the index of belief $r = 1$) that the most familiar characters are adjectives with positive meaning; the subject's evaluation of these characters can be considered to be a projection of the subject's state onto a segment 0-6.

Let us consider now one of the most surprising experiments in the investigation of 'mere exposure' (Kunst-Wilson & Zajonc, 1980). The subjects were shown twenty irregular octagons arbitrary divided for each subject in two sets of ten. At the first stage of the experiment, the ten octagons of one set were presented to a subject one by one (five times each) with a very short exposition time (a few milliseconds). With such short exposition, a subject cannot consciously distinguish one object from the other. If asked what he sees, the subject would indicate a grayish, slightly glimmering background. At the second stage, the subjects were presented with the pairs of octagons: one 'old' (shown at the first stage) and one new, but were not told that some of the octagons had been presented earlier. With no time limitation, each subject had a task to choose the octagon which he likes more. It turned out that the frequency of choosing the octagons presented during the first phase was equal to 0.60.

We have analyzed data of the similar experiments conducted by other researchers and found the following frequencies for choosing the shapes presented earlier:

Seamon et al. (1983)	0.61
Mandler et al. (1987)	0.62
Bonnano et al. (1986)	0.66, 0.63, 0.62, 0.61, 0.63, 0.62

We can see that all numbers are grouped around 0.62. A phenomenon of the appearance of 0.62 can be explained as follows. The shapes that were presented have no property based on which the subject's cognitive system could compute x_1 and x_2. Therefore, the subject can be considered autonomous. A pair of octagons played the role of a screen, and the pole of belief, beyond the subject's consciousness, proved to become the shape seen *earlier*. Since no emotional pressure was rendered, the index of belief $r = 1$, and the subjects choose the shape presented earlier with the frequency of the golden section value.

The experiments described in this section support our hypothesis formulated in the first edition of this book (see Conclusion): in this kind of experiments, the frequency of choosing the pole of belief numerically coincides with normalized categorical evaluations and is equal to the golden section value.

PART VI
CATEGORIZATION OF SELF AND OTHERS WITH THE HELP OF BIPOLAR CONSTRUCTS

6.1. Historical Excursus

Research in this area has led to the discovery that the frequency of 0.62 has a special persistence in statistics of binary choice. Systematic studies of subjects' evaluations of other people were pioneered by Kelly (1955). The essence of his view is that a person uses a system of bipolar evaluations for mental representations of the self and other people. Kelly elaborated refined methods for the extraction of individual sets of bipolar constructs from subjects. He assumed that such constructs must be symmetrical with regard to positive and negative poles, that is, that people would choose positive and negative poles with approximately the same frequency. This assumption, however, proved to be mistaken: on the average, subjects chose a positive pole significantly more often than the negative one.

Kelly's studies were continued by his followers, Adams-Webber and Benjafield. In the early 1970s, they came to the conclusion not only that subjects choose the positive pole more often than the negative one, but also that there is a particular frequency of this choice: 0.62 (Adams-Webber & Benjafield, 1973). In 1976, they put forth the hypothesis that the precise value of this frequency is equal to the "magic" golden section (Benjafield & Adams-Webber, 1976). The experimental work in this area was done by a number of different researchers: Adams-Webber (1979, 1982, 1984, 1985a, 1985b), Benjafield (1984), Benjafield & Green (1978), Schwartz & Garamoni (1986), Schwartz & Michelson (1987), Romany & Adams-Webber (1981), Rigdon & Epting (1982), Messick (1987), Marczewska

(1983), Tuohy (1987), Tuohy & Stradling (1987). All of this research confirms the hypothesis that in evaluating other people subjects chose the positive pole of a bipolar construct with the frequency 0.60-0.64.

Vladimir Lefebvre (1985) has suggested that the precise value of the golden section appears when subjects evaluate inanimate objects rather than people, proposing a formal model of the subject. In a subsequent publication (Lefebvre, V.A., Lefebvre, V.D., & Adams-Webber, 1986), the authors elaborated a more general model. With the help of this model they attempted to explain the set of data obtained through experiments in which the subjects categorized their acquaintances. At that time a formal analogue for 'belief' had not yet been introduced and the model appeared unwieldy.

In this chapter we propose another explanation for Adams-Webber's experimental data based on the concepts described in this book.

6.2. The Experiments of Adams-Webber

The objective of these experiments was to investigate the relation between subjects' self-evaluation and their evaluation of other people (Adams-Webber, 1979, 1985a,b; Adams-Webber & Rodney, 1983). First, the subject created a list of his acquaintances using special instructions based on the so-called repertoire method. For example, the subject had to include in the list the name of one person with whom he recently became acquainted and wanted to know better; the name of a person with whom he felt uncomfortable; and so on. Then the subject was given a set of twelve constructs and asked to evaluate himself and each of the acquaintances in terms of these constructs. The set was elaborated in accordance with Osgood's semantical differential (Osgood, Suci, & Tannenbaum, 1957): (1) generous-stingy, (2) pleasant-unpleasant, (3) true-false, (4) fair-unfair, (5) active-passive, (6) energetic-lethargic, (7) sharp-dull, (8) excitable-calm, (9) strong-weak, (10) bold-timid, (11) hard-soft, (12) rugged-delicate.

The experiments were conducted under three different 'moods' induced in the subjects according to special instructions. The instructions for 'a neutral mood' contained only technical explanations of how to register the evaluations. The instructions for the 'positive mood' encouraged the subject to imagine himself very successful (for example, he received straight A's on his exams, found a summer good job, learned that his girlfriend is in love with him). The instructions for a 'negative mood' ask the subject to imagine himself a failure (he has failed all his exams except one, cannot find a summer job, has learned that his girlfriend is leaving him).

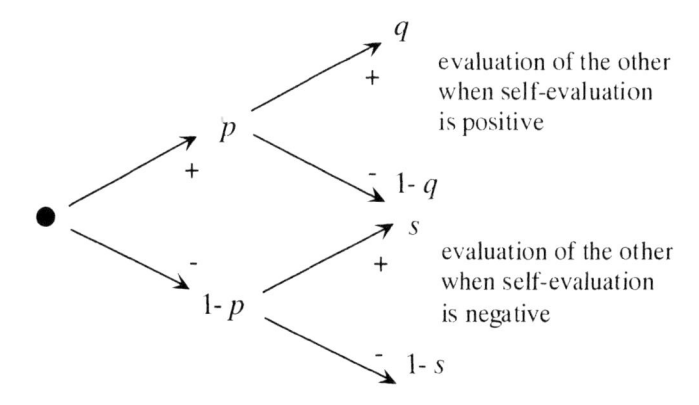

Fig. 6.2.1. A graph corresponding to the three-member set (p, q, s).

p is the frequency of the subject's positive evaluation of the self; q is the frequency of the subject's positive evaluation of others according to constructs giving positive self-evaluation; s is the frequency of the subject's positive evaluation of others according to constructs giving negative self-evaluation.

Thus, separate experimental data were obtained for neutral, positive, and negative moods. For each mood a set of three numbers (p, q, s) was found: p is the frequency of positive self-evaluations, q is the frequency of positive evaluations of others on those constructs for which self-evaluations are positive, and s is the frequency of positive evaluations of others on those constructs for which self-evaluation was negative. Each set (p, q, s) corresponds to the graph given on Fig.6.2.1.

Adams-Webber and his colleagues conducted three independent series of such experiments, the results of which are given in Table 6.2.1.

Table 6.2.1
Results of the experiments of Adams-Webber
with theoretical predictions given in rectangular frames

mood	frequency of positive self-evaluation	frequency of positive evaluation of others on those constructs for which self-evaluation is	
		positive	negative
neutral	0.77 0.73 0.73 0.75	0.67 0.67 0.68 0.67	0.50 0.48 0.52 0.50
positive	0.83 0.81 0.78 0.80	0.70 0.72 0.74 0.75	0.46 0.45 0.50 0.50
negative	0.63 0.53 0.60	0.62 0.58 0.60	0.56 0.53 0.50

6.3. A Model of the Process of Self-Evaluation

Let us look at the constructs given in section 6.2. They are not operational; that is, the subject does not have an objective criterion which would give him grounds to ascribe a pole to the self. Because of this, his decisions are based on belief, and we can put him in correspondence with equation (4.2.9). We assume that a pole of belief $\alpha = $ *I'm good*.

The data in Table 6.2.1 allow us to presume that with a neutral mood the subject's index of belief during self-evaluation is $R = 2$; we can see from (4.2.9) that in this case $X_1 = 0.75$. With a positive mood the index of belief is $R = 3$; it follows from (4.2.9) that in this case $X_1 = 0.80$. And with negative mood $R < 1$ and seems to be quite unstable, because in one experiment the frequency of positive evaluation was 0.63, and in the other 0.53. In constructing Table 6.2.1, we consider $R = 1/2$ in the negative mood, which means $X_1 = 0.60$.

6.4. A Model of the Process of Evaluation of Others

In evaluating other people the subject relies on belief for the same reason as in evaluating the self. *Suppose that the mechanism for evaluation of others is the same as that for self-evaluation.* Then we can again put the subject in correspondence with equation (4.2.9) and consider a pole of belief α = *He (she) is good.* Let us introduce the following assumptions:

(1) If the subject evaluates himself positively in the terms of a certain construct, then in a neutral mood the index of belief during the evaluation of others in the terms of the same construct is $R = 1$, in a positive mood $R = 2$, and in a negative mood $R = 1/2$.

(2) If the subject evaluates himself negatively in the terms of a particular construct, then the index of belief during the evaluation of others in the terms of the same construct is $R = 0$, regardless of the mood.

It follows from equation (4.2.9) that for a positive self-evaluation, the positivity of others is:

in a neutral mood, $X_1 = 2/3 \approx 0.67$
in a positive mood, $X_1 = 3/4 = 0.75$
in a negative mood, $X_1 = 3/5 = 0.60$.

In addition, it follows from (4.2.9) that with negative self-evaluation, when $R = 0$ independently of the mood, $X = 0.50$. These figures are given in Table 6.2.1 in rectangular frames.

6.5. The Probability of Positive Evaluation of Another Person

Let us find now the probability of the positive evaluation of another person when the subject is in a neutral mood. This value is as follows (see Fig.6.2.1):

$$q^+ = pq + (1 - p)s = (0.75)(0.67) + (0.25)(0.5) \approx 0.63.$$

We can accept the possibility that under certain conditions the subjects may depersonify other people and, as a result, evaluate them according to the schema for inanimate objects. In such a case the theoretical value for the frequency of positive choices at a neutral mood ought to be exactly equal to the golden section.

6.6. An Experiment by Grice et al.

Grice et al. (2005) recently repeated Adams-Webber's (1979) experiments for the neutral mood using another method. Grice's data are given in Table 6.6.1 along with numbers predicted by our model.

We see that although all predictions are very close to experimental data numerically, only positive self-evaluation is within 95% CI. We can hypothesize that in the real experiments, there are factors which our model does not take into consideration.

Table 6.6.1.

Data obtained in the experiment by Grice et al. and the model predictions

	Predicted	Observed	95% CI
Positive self-evaluations	0.75	0.757	0.735, 0.778
Positive other evaluations when self is positive	0.667	0.647*	0.640, 0.653
Positive other evaluations when self is negative	0.5	0.517*	0.505, 0.529

Note. * indicates observed proportion is significantly different from predicted proportion ($p < 0.05$, two sided).

PART VII
NATURAL GENERATION
OF GEOMETRICAL PROPORTIONS

7.1. Historical Excursus

Since ancient times it has been believed that the Golden Section possesses a special aesthetic value. Indeed, research has shown that the golden section was used in ancient cultures more often than other ratios (Hambidge, 1920; Colman & Coan, 1920; Doczi, 1981). The ratio $\sqrt{2}/2 \approx 0.707$ is a distant second. Ghyka (1946) cites the measurements of one hundred and twenty ancient vases from the Boston Museum: it turns out that the contour of 96 vases is based on the golden section, 18 on ratio $\sqrt{2}/2$, and 6 on ratio close to $\sqrt{3}/3$. The artists of the Renaissance, including Leonardo da Vinci (Archibald, 1920), also used the golden section ratio as did contemporary architects like Le Corbusier (1968).

Fechner (1876) was the first who tried to examine experimentally the attractiveness of the golden section. Subjects were given a set of ten rectangles with sides whose ratios varied between 1/1 and 2/5. Their task was to indicate the most and the least attractive rectangle. Fechner found that the most attractive was that rectangle the ratio of whose sides was equal to the golden section. These results were supported by Lalo (1908). Later studies, however, demonstrated that the choice of the most attractive rectangle is not stable and depends on the conditions of the experiment (Davis, 1933; Thompson, 1946; Shipley, Daltman, & Steele, 1947; and Berlyne, 1971). In addition, Godkewitsch (1974) and Piehl (1976) have found that this choice depends on the range of side ratios presented to the subjects (see also the discussion of this problem in Plug, 1980; Benjafield, 1985; and Valentine, 1965).

Most of the experiments mentioned above have one feature in common: the subjects have to choose one object from a set. If, however, we consider experiments in which the subjects were asked to construct a nice looking object, instead of choosing it, we find quite different results. Svensson (1977) asked his subjects to draw five vertical and five horizontal lines of various lengths and then to put a dot on each line so that the ratio looked attractive. The distribution he obtained has a maximum close to the golden section.

Another approach was employed by Benjafield, Pomeroy, and Saunders (1980). They demonstrated those mistakes in reproducing the golden section are significantly smaller than those in reproducing the ratios 2/3 and 3/4, and equal to that for 1/2.

It is necessary to note that the experiments by Schiffman & Bobko (1978), Plug (1980), as well as Davis & Jahnke (1991), in which subjects were induced to generate a ratio, did not support the hypothesis about the golden section.

With the exception of observations done by Davis (1933), we have found no experimental data supporting the attractiveness of the ratio $\sqrt{2}/2$. Davis' subjects had to draw rectangles with a maximally attractive ratio of sides. Davis notes that $\sqrt{2}/2$ corresponds to one of the local maximums in the distribution of ratios obtained in this experiment.

All of these investigations seem to lead us to the conclusion that the special attractiveness of the golden section is just a myth hallowed by tradition. Recently, however, Lockhead (1989) created an experimental method allowing him to separate the golden section from all other ratios.

7.2. Lockhead's Method

The essence of this method is as follows. A subject is given a piece of paper with two dots. The instructions say: "Imagine that there is a dot in the middle between the two dots above. Now, using your pencil, move the imaginary dot toward the left (right) until you can just begin to feel that the two dots on the left (right) belong together as a 'group' while the one on the right (left) is by itself. Place the dot at this point." (Lockhead, 1989, p.272)

It has turned out that on the average the subjects divide the segment between the dots in such a way that the ratio of new segments is close to the golden section.

We have extracted similar results from Bigava's data (1979). He had 708 subjects; the task was to move a handle in a vertical slot to a certain height, after which the handle was returned to its initial position and the subject was asked to perform exactly half of his original movement. Our recalculations have demonstrated that, on average, the subjects stopped on a spot higher than the center, 0.615 of the length, that is, they divided the line into the golden section ratio.

7.3. The Golden Section in Generation of Geometrical Proportions as a Result of Projecting the Subject's State onto a Segment

We will assume that in generating geometrical proportions an artist can be considered an autonomous subject whose activity is directed toward an external object (see sections 2.3). Therefore, we can put the subject in correspondence with equation (4.3.5). Suppose that in Lockhead's experiment $r = 1$. Then the theoretical length of the projection of the subject's state onto a scale is equal exactly to the golden section.

The difficulties connected with verifying various hypotheses on the golden section seem to be inherent in the problem itself. At the end of section 8.8 we will see that the projection of the golden section onto a scale may involve deviation of up to 0.049.

PART VIII
NATURAL GENERATION OF MUSICAL INTERVALS

8.1. Historical Excursus

The nature of musical intervals has long concerned musicologists and constitutes one of man's oldest scientific problems. About five hundred B.C. the Pythagoreans established a relationship between the pitch produced by two strings and a ratio of natural numbers (see, for example, McClain, 1976). The Pythagoreans stated the principle that the source of musical harmony lies in the world of natural numbers. To illustrate this principle, we may use Plato's metaphor and say that the aural experience of strings' lengths is only a shadow of their fundamental arithmetic ratios. This mode of thinking led to concrete results: Pythagorean tuning was created, based on the postulate that only the numbers 1, 2, and 3 are perfect, as are ratios whose members are exponents with the bases 2 and 3.

Table 8.1.1 shows the main intervals of Pythagorean tuning. Let us note that the selection of these ratios as basic was not suggested by empirical study. It was done according to the general Pythagorean picture of the Universum, in which a concept of ideal ratios dominated.

Pythagorean tuning was used in European musical culture up to the fourteenth century, when the gradual development of polyphony led to the introduction of thirds (4/5 and 5/6) and sixths (5/8 and 3/5) (Cohen, 1984). After that, the problem of why musical ratios are ratios of integers was considered in the context of attempts to provide a strict mathematical definition of consonance. The key figures in these studies were Gioseffo Zarlino (1517-1590), Simon Stevin (1548-1620), and Johanes Kepler (1571-1630). One practical result of this period was the creation of the Just

Table 8.1.1
Interval Comparison in Different Mathematical Tuning System*

	Pythagorean Tuning (PT)			Just Intonation (JI)		
Interval name	Numeric origin	Frequency ratio	cents	Numeric origin	Frequency ratio	cents
Unison	1 : 1	1.000	0.0	1 : 1	1.000	0.0
Minor Second	$3^5 : 2^8$ $2^{11} : 3^7$	0.949 0.936	90.2 113.7	15 : 16	0.937	111.7
Major Second	$2^3 : 3^2$	0.889	203.9	9 : 10 8 : 9 7 : 8	0.900 0.889 0.875	182.4 203.9 231.2
Minor Third	$3^3 : 2^5$ $2^{14} : 3^9$	0.844 0.832	294.1 317.6	5 : 6	0.833	315.6
Major Third	$2^6 : 3^4$	0.791	407.8	4 : 5	0.800	386.3
Fourth	$3 : 2^2$	0.750	498.1	3 : 4	0.750	498.1
Triton	$3^6 : 2^{10}$ $2^9 : 3^6$	0.712 0.702	588.3 611.7	32 : 45 45 : 64	0.711 0.703	590.2 609.8
Fifth	2 : 3	0.667	702.0	2 : 3	0.667	702.0
Minor Sixth	$3^4 : 2^7$ $2^{12} : 3^8$	0.631 0.624	792.2 815.6	5 : 8	0.625	813.7
Major Sixth	$2^4 : 3^3$	0.593	905.0	3 : 5	0.600	884.4
Minor Seventh	$3^2 : 2^4$	0.562	996.1	4 : 7 9 : 16	0.571 0.562	968.8 996.1
Major Seventh	$2^{15} : 3^{10}$ $2^7 : 3^5$	0.555 0.526	1019.1 1109.8	5 : 9 8 : 15	0.555 0.533	1017.6 1088.3
Octave	1 : 2	0.500	1200.0	1 : 2	0.500	1200.0

*This table was constructed on the base of the table in Burns & Ward (1982). We have supplemented it with our reconstruction of Pelog intervals,

Table 8.1.1 (cont.)

	Pelog (Pel)			Equal Temperament (ET)	
Interval name	Numeric origin	Frequency ratio	cents	Frequency ratio	cents
Unison	1 : 1	1.000	0.0	1.000	0.0
Minor Second	15 : 16	0.937	111.7	0.944	100
Major Second	9 : 10 7 : 8 6 : 7	0.900 0.875 0.857	182.4 231.2 266.9	0.891	200
Minor Third	5 : 6	0.833	315.6	0.841	300
Major Third	4 : 5	0.800	386.3	0.794	400
Fourth	3 : 4	0.750	498.1	0.749	500
Triton				0.707	600
Fifth	2 : 3	0.667	702.0	0.668	700
Minor Sixth	5 : 8	0.625	813.7	0.630	800
Major Sixth	3 : 5 7 : 12	0.600 0.583	884.4 923.1	0.595	900
Minor Seventh	4 : 7	0.571	968.8		
Major Seventh	5 : 9 8 : 15	0.555 0.533	1017.6 1088.3	0.561 0.530	1000 1100
Octave	1 : 2	0.500	1200.0	0.500	1200

Intonation set (see Table 8.1.1), on which the tempered scale was later based. Recently, McClain (1976) has made the astonishing discovery that the set of proportions equivalent to the entire Just Intonation set of intervals had been known to Plato. All these ratios are encoded in the proportions of the number of inhabitants in the various sectors of Plato's model of the City of Magnesia described in The Law. (See also McClain, 1987, and Lefebvre, 1987b, 1989.)

The rationalist revolution in science that began in the sixteenth century affected also musicology. The new generation of scholars was not satisfied with reducing harmonic ratios to arithmetical ones. Vincento Galilei (1520-1591) and his son Galileo Galilei (1564-1642) were among the first to introduce the problem of consonance into the sphere of physics. Galileo Galilei substituted physical schemas for arithmetical ones; he pioneered the study of vibrations, sketching out a 'theory of coincidences' in which he made a first step toward the contemporary theory of resonance.

The further development of such explanatory schemes is connected with mathematical physics (Newton, I., Bernoulli, D., Euler, D'Alambert). This line reached its apogee in the works of Joseph Fourier (1768-1830), who demonstrated that the oscillations of a string can be represented as the superposition of elementary sinusoid oscillations whose frequency ratios are related to each other as integers. At that time it seemed that the explanation of why musical intervals are ratios of integers lay concealed in the laws of resonance. Hermann von Helmholtz (1821-1894) succeeded in relating a physical picture of oscillations to the nature of human hearing (Helmholtz, 1877). Helmholtz assumed that the aesthetic characteristics of intervals were connected with beatings produced by overtones. In this view, the most euphonious intervals should be the unison, octave, perfect fifth, and perfect fourth. Krueger (1910) modified Helmholtz's theory, taking into consideration the phenomenon of dissonant beats appearing between difference tones. Helmholtz's theory was further developed by Plomp & Levelt (1965).

Let us note that Helmholtz's theory was not the only psychoacoustic theory in existence at the turn of the twentieth century. Among competing approaches was the theory of Lipps (1905), who tried to demonstrate that the human psyche has its own microrhythms and that the phenomenon of consonance is connected with the coincidence of physical and psychological rhythms. There was also the work of Stumpf (1883), who proposed what he called a theory of fusion to explain the phenomenon of two sounds' joining into one during the perception of consonance. The problem of integer ratios, apart from a few gaps, seemed to be resolved.

In the middle of the twentieth century, however, the discussion flared up again. The problem is that psychoacoustics offer more or less plausible explanations only for the euphony of integer intervals in harmonic structures. It does not help us to understand why melodic structures use the same ratios (see Ward, 1954, 1962; Ward & Martin, 1961; Elfner, 1964; Krumhansl & Shepard, 1979; Meyer, 1962a,b).

> A certain degree of preference for simple ratios is understandable when one is dealing with simultaneous tones that are intense enough to produce beats. However, when applied to tones heard alternately the argument that simple ratios are preferred is simply numerological nonsense. (Ward, 1963, p.679)

An attempt to salvage the theory of integer ratios was made by Terhardt (1974), who tried to create a synthesis of psychoacoustics and Gestalt theory. In spite of this, belief in the integer basis of musical intervals was completely broken, and the newest cognitive theories of music perception deliberately avoid the idea of integer ratios (see, for example, Shepard, 1982a, 1982b). We will cite here the words of Richard Feynman:

> We may question whether we are any better off than Pythagoras in understanding why only certain sounds are pleasant to our ear. The general theory of aesthetics is probably no further advanced now than in the time of Pythagoras. (Feynman et al., 1966, p.50-l)

Let us now look more closely at the analysis of musical intervals made by Pythagoras himself. Musical categories corresponding to the octave, fifth, and fourth were used long before him. As far as we know, no one connected them with ratios of natural numbers. Nevertheless musicians used them, and they knew the specific peculiarity of their sounds. Pythagoras' theory fundamentally changed the approach to intervals: they began to be categorized according to mathematical ratios instead of the peculiarity of their sounds. The words 'interval' and 'ratio' even became synonymous. Generations passed; scientific schools were born and died, but the principle of categorizing musical intervals by means of mathematical ratios remained unchanged.

There does exist, however, another approach: first, pairs of tones are categorized according to the individuality of their sounds; then, for each individuality, singled out, the range of ratios within which this individuality still remains, is delineated. It seems that the first to explore this route consistently was the Russian musicologist and psychoacoustician N.A. Garbuzov (1880-1955). He introduced the concept of musical zones and demonstrated experimentally that the individuality of intervals relates not to a single ratio but rather to a segment on a musical scale (Garbuzov, 1948):

> If we gradually change the size of a tempered minor third, increasing or decreasing it within the bounds of 30 cents (approximately), we will continue to perceive it as the interval of a minor third (the zone of stable reading). Then, if we further increase or decrease the interval within the bounds of 12 cents (approximately) we will perceive an interval of an uncertain individuality, a mixture either of a major and minor third or of a minor third and major second. Comparable phenomena can be observed through examination of other intervals. (Garbuzov, 1990, p.150)

Let us emphasize once more that Garbuzov defines an interval by its individuality, not its frequency ratio. Therefore one interval (in the example given, a minor third) corresponds to a certain range of ratios. Thus depending on which particular ratio of frequencies is chosen we can obtain different qualitative versions of the same interval (zone). Garbuzov calls them 'intonations'. He believed that zone tuning consists of 'unlimited sets' of intonational versions, and that each performance of a musical piece in zone tuning by human voices or musical instruments is a "unique intonational version of a performance." Garbuzov suggested creating a new zone-type theory of musical acoustics to replace the traditional one which he called dot-acoustics because each interval corresponds to only one dot on the musical scale. He believed also that the twelve-zone musical system appeared not as merely artificial convention, but rather the natural development of musical culture led to aural selection of zones with a particular degree of individuality.

In other words, Garbuzov presumed that diatonic scales appeared as the result of categorizing certain interval zones with specific psychoacoustic properties. If this is true, such a zone must be cross-culturally valid. Unfortunately, Garbuzov's works remained unknown to Western musicologists, no experiments were conducted to verify them, and his concepts did not enter the intellectual bank of Western musicological thought. Moreover, an opposed way of thinking dominates Western musicology: the idea that the categorization of intervals in a given culture predetermines the character of their perception, and not vice versa (see Dowling & Harwood, 1986).

There have been many theoretical and experimental works concerned - both pro and contra - with the assumed universality of diatonic scales. Balzano (1980) brought formal algebraic arguments to support the idea of universality, demonstrating that diatonic tempered scales have advantages over others with respect to their possibilities for melodic transposition. Trehub (1987) conducted experiments on infants' ability to perceive various aspects of musical material and demonstrated that the "diatonic context has greater coherence or stability for infants than does the non-diatonic" (Trehub, 1987, p.638).

Krumhansl & Jusczyk (1990) conducted an experiment in which babies listened to sections of Mozart minuets divided into segments that either did or did not correspond to the phrase structure of the music. The babies listened significantly longer to the appropriately segmented versions.

By contrast, Lynch et al. (1990) compared babies' reactions to melodies based on native western major, western minor, and non-native Javanese Pelog scales. No significant differences in the babies' responses were found. Thus, from the experimental point of view, the question of cross-cultural validity for diatonic scales has no solution as yet.

To sum up, we may distinguish three different points of view on the nature of musical intervals:

1. Music uses proportions of pitches which are close to the ratios of small natural numbers.

2. There is a universal cross-cultural categorization of pairs of tones, such that each category corresponds to a continuous zone of frequency ratios.

3. The sizes of intervals are not fundamental values. They are predetermined by the general structure of a given musical system.

In this chapter we will demonstrate that viewpoints 1 and 2 are both true and do not contradict each other. In addition, we will formally deduce the Just Intonation and Pelog sets from our model and put forth a hypothesis that the function of musical intervals consists in a transferal of an emotional state from one subject to another.

8.2. Musical Intervals as Projections of States

A musical interval can be considered a projection of the subject's state onto a screen, whose unit corresponds to the lower tone and whose projection corresponds to the higher tone (see section 2.3).

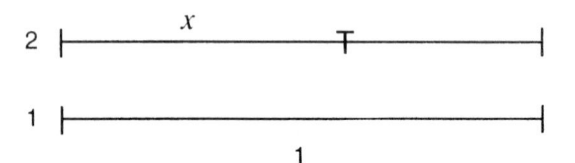

Fig. 8.2.1. An abstract two-stringed instrument.

In Fig.8.2.1 string 1 generates the lower tone, and the active part of string 2 (from the left margin to the movable bridge T) generates the higher tone. If we assume the length of strings be equal to 1, then the length x of the active part of string 2 will be equal to the value of the musical interval generated by the two strings with fixed position of a bridge.

We presume that during the generation of musical intervals the subject is autonomous (see Part IV) and that his state is predetermined by the value $R = D/s$, which corresponds to the case in which the subject's activity is focused on the self (see section 2.3). Thus, we can put the following equation into correspondence with a musician:

$$X = \frac{R+1}{R+2}, \qquad (8.2.1)$$

where R is equal either to k or $1/k$, $k = 1, 2, \ldots$. This equation corresponds to possible states of the subject during his creation of musical intervals. Because we consider the musical interval a projection of the subject's state, we have to assume $x = X$.

Let us substitute values for R and X and derive two equations:

$$x = \frac{k+1}{k+2}, \qquad (8.2.2)$$

$$x = \frac{k+1}{2k+1}. \qquad (8.2.3)$$

The equations (8.2.2) and (8.2.3) correspond to the intervals which the subject can generate.

8.3. Elite Intervals

The intervals 1/1 (unison) and 1/2 (octave) are the limits of sequences (8.2.2) and (8.2.3) when $k \to \infty$. Let us add these two intervals to the intervals of the type (8.2.2) and (8.2.3) and call the set of intervals so obtained the *set of elite intervals* (Lefebvre, 1987a). We see that the perfect fifth (2/3) is a special case within this set: it corresponds to the state of balance, because in this case $R = 1$.

8.4. Formal Deduction of the Just Intonation Set

The next structural unit in music after an interval is a triad of tones. Let us consider all possible triads which contain the perfect fifth (2/3). In order to realize such triads on our abstract instrument, we give it one more string with a bridge in fixed position 2/3 of the way from the left end (Fig.8.4.1).

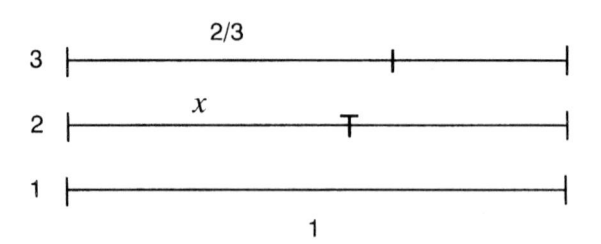

Fig. 8.4.1. An abstract three-stringed instrument.

Let our theoretical musician generate only elite intervals. Imagine now that he hits all three strings (consecutively or simultaneously). Which values of x does he have to choose in order for all the intervals generated to be elite? The interval between the strings 1 and 3 is 2/3. The interval between the strings 1 and 2 is equal to $x/1 = x$. We designate the interval between strings 2 and 3 as y: if $x > 2/3$, then $y = 2/3x$, if $x < 2/3$, then $y = 3x/2$; and if $x = 2/3$, then $y = 1/1$. It is easy to verify that for each interval x, equal to

$$\frac{1}{2} \quad \frac{2}{3} \quad \frac{1}{1}, \qquad (8.4.1)$$

the corresponding triad contains only elite intervals.

Let $1/2 < x < 1$, $x \neq 2/3$, and k_1, and k_2 are natural numbers. In order that all three intervals constituting a triad be elite, x must satisfy one of the two systems of equations:

for $\frac{2}{3} < x < 1$,
$$\left. \begin{array}{l} x = \dfrac{k_1 + 1}{k_1 + 2} \\[6pt] y = \dfrac{k_2 + 1}{k_2 + 2} \\[6pt] y = \dfrac{2}{3x} \end{array} \right\}, \qquad (8.4.2)$$

for $\frac{1}{2} < x < \frac{2}{3}$,
$$\left.\begin{array}{l} x = \dfrac{k_1 + 1}{2k_1 + 1} \\ y = \dfrac{k_2 + 1}{k_2 + 2} \\ y = \dfrac{3x}{2} \end{array}\right\} . \qquad (8.4.3)$$

These systems follow from equations (8.2.2) and (8.2.3), the definition of y, and the analogy of equation (8.2.2) for y. The latter exists in both systems because $y > 2/3$. By excluding x and y from systems (8.4.2) and (8.4.3) we obtain two Diophantine equations:

$$k_1 = \frac{k_2 + 5}{k_2 - 1}, \quad k_2 > 1, \qquad (8.4.4)$$

$$k_1 = \frac{k_2 + 4}{k_2 - 2}, \quad k_2 > 2. \qquad (8.4.5)$$

Let us solve equation (8.4.4). If $m = k_2 - 1$, then

$$k_1 = 1 + \frac{6}{m}. \qquad (8.4.6)$$

Since k_2 is a natural number, m can take on only the values of integral divisors of 6; that is, $m = 1, 2, 3,$ and 6. Therefore,

$$k_1 = 2, 3, 4, 7. \qquad (8.4.7)$$

Substituting these values for k_1 in the first equation of system (8.4.2) we obtain the following set of intervals:

$$\frac{3}{4} \quad \frac{4}{5} \quad \frac{5}{6} \quad \frac{8}{9}. \qquad (8.4.8)$$

Now solve equation (8.4.5). Let $m = k_2 - 2$; the result is again equation (8.4.6), from which we obtain the set of values (8.4.7) for k_1. Substituting these values for k_1 in the first equation of system (8.4.3) we obtain the following intervals

$$\frac{3}{5} \quad \frac{4}{7} \quad \frac{5}{9} \quad \frac{8}{15}. \qquad (8.4.9)$$

We will call the intervals (8.4.1), (8.4.8), and (8.4.9) *superelite*. Now let us find octave complements x' for each superelite interval x (the relation between the intervals x and x' is defined by the equation $x'x = 1/2$). Octave complements necessarily appear during the construction of a musical scale based on the octave. Given below are all the superelite intervals and those octave complements which are not superelite:

superelite intervals	$\frac{1}{2}$	$\frac{8}{15}$	$\frac{5}{9}$	$\frac{4}{7}$	$\frac{3}{5}$	$\frac{2}{3}$	$\frac{3}{4}$	$\frac{4}{5}$	$\frac{5}{6}$	$\frac{8}{9}$	$\frac{1}{1}$
octave complements		$\frac{15}{16}$	$\frac{9}{10}$	$\frac{7}{8}$				$\frac{5}{8}$		$\frac{9}{16}$	

From Table 8.1.1 we can see that the set obtained coincides with the Just Intonation set, without the interval 32/45 and its octave complement 45/64. Interval $32/45 \approx 0.711$ is a famous tritone (see Table 8.1.1) which symbolized the appearance of the devil in the operas of the eighteen and nineteen centuries. In musicologists' works this interval stands apart from all others. Let us emphasize that we deduced the Just Intonation set without recourse to psychoacoustics.

8.5. Major and Minor Triads

Among natural scales the best known are the *major* and *minor* scales. These scales can be shown in tables, using columns and lines to represent tones and their intersections to represent intervals (see Table 8.5.1). Each scale has a basic triad which is at the core of melodic and harmonic structures performed in its key. For *C-major* it is *C-E-G*, and for *C-minor* it is $C\text{-}E^\flat\text{-}G$. Why are those particular triads basic? To answer this question, assume that the importance of each tone is defined by the number of elite intervals generated through it. This number is equal to the number of elite intervals in a column (or in a line) corresponding to that particular tone. All these numbers, computed along columns, are given in the lowest lines of Tables 8.5.1A and 8.5.1B. We can see that in *C-major*, *C*, *E*, and *G* have the greatest numbers; in *C-minor* it is *C*, E^b, and *G*. Thus, starting from the hypothesis that the importance of a tone in a scale is defined by the number of the elite intervals generated with it, it follows that triads *C-E-G* and *C-E^b-G* consist of the leading tones in each scale. This predetermines the dominated role of these two triads in relation to other triads, since each of them, when sounding together with other tones of its scale, generates fewer non-elite intervals than any other triad from the same scale. We can see from tables 8.5.1A and 8.5.1B that the *C-major* triad does not generate non-elite intervals at all, and that the *C-minor* triad generates only one non-elite interval, $C-A^b$.

8.6. Psychological Profiles of Major and Minor

The hypothesis that the importance of a tone in a scale is defined by the number of elite intervals it generates can be verified experimentally. The essence of these experiments must consist of musicians' judgments of the extent to which each tone in a major and minor scale fits other elements of the scale. An experiment of this type was conducted by Krumhansl & Kessler (1982) (without any relation to our model). The subjects with some musical training were asked to listen to major (or minor) chords and cadences and then to a single tone chosen at random from the set of the tones of the chromatic scale. The subjects' task was to mark on a seven-point scale "how well, in a musical sense, each probe tone fit into or went with the musical element just heard. On this scale, 1 was designated 'fits poorly' and 7 was designated 'fits well', and subjects were encouraged to use the full range of the response scale." (Krumhansl & Kessler, 1982, p.342)

Figure 8.6.1 illustrates the close correspondences between the profiles predicted by our model and the major and minor profiles obtained in these experiments.

Table 8.5.1 A
Intervals corresponding to the C-major scale

	C	D	E	F	G	A	B
C	1	8/9	4/5	3/4	2/3	3/5	8/15
D	8/9	1	9/10	27/32*	3/4	27/40*	3/5
E	4/5	9/10	1	15/16	5/6	3/4	2/3
F	3/4	27/32*	15/16	1	8/9	4/5	32/45*
G	2/3	3/4	5/6	8/9	1	9/10	4/5
A	3/5	27/40*	3/4	4/5	9/10	1	8/9
B	8/15	3/5	2/3	32/45*	4/5	8/9	1
	7	5	7	5	7	6	6

Table 8.5.1 B
Intervals corresponding to the C-minor scale

	C	D	E^b	F	G	A^b	B^b
C	1	8/9	5/6	3/4	2/3	5/8*	5/9
D	8/9	1	15/16	27/32*	3/4	45/64*	5/8*
E^b	5/6	15/16	1	9/10	4/5	3/4	2/3
F	3/4	27/32*	9/10	1	8/9	5/6	20/27*
G	2/3	3/4	4/5	8/9	1	15/16	5/6
A^b	5/8*	45/64*	3/4	5/6	15/16	1	8/9
B^b	5/9	5/8*	2/3	20/27*	5/6	8/9	1
	6	4	7	5	7	5	5

* Non-elite intervals

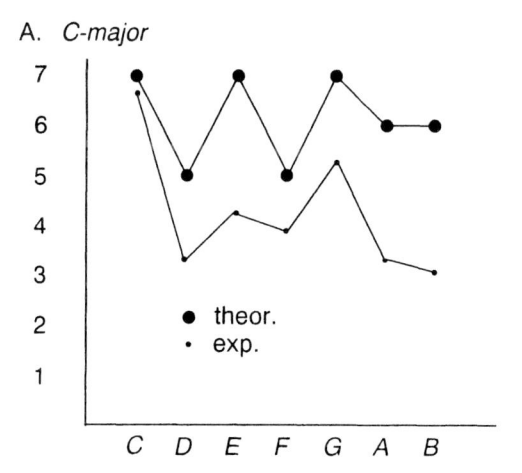

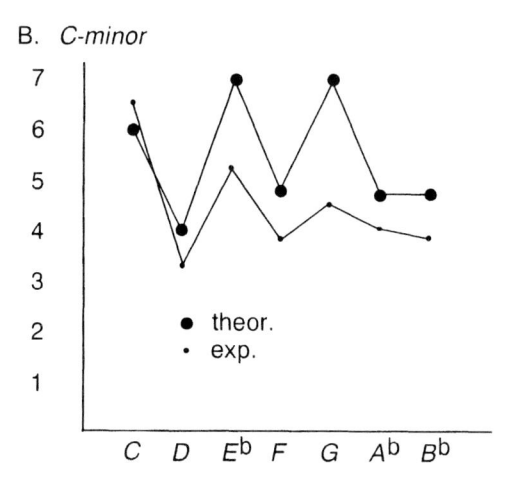

Fig. 8.6.1. Graphs of experimental and theoretical profiles for *C*-major and *C*-minor.

Each experimental value corresponds to a mean of estimations (on a 7-point scale) obtained for a single tone (based on data from Krumhansl, 1990, Table 2.1, p.30). Each theoretical value corresponds to the number of elite intervals which contain a given tone (see Table 8.5.1).

8.7. Pelog

We have attempted to reconstruct the musical system Pelog from the island of Java (Lefebvre, 1992; Lefebvre & Garfias, 1991). Our analysis of the Pelog system, based on Kunst's data (Kunst, 1949), demonstrates that it is produced by the perfect fourth (3/4) in the same sense as Just Intonation is produced by the perfect fifth. In order to find the intervals of the Pelog system, one must substitute a string of the length 3/4 in Fig.8.4.1 for the string of the length 2/3 and find the values of x, such that all three intervals are elite. With direct computation we find that for x equal to

$$\frac{1}{2} \quad \frac{3}{4} \quad \frac{1}{1}, \tag{8.7.1}$$

the corresponding triads consist of only elite intervals. By designating the interval between strings 2 and 3 as y (as it was done for the fifth), we obtain two systems of Diophantine equations:

for $\frac{3}{4} < x < 1$,
$$\left. \begin{array}{l} x = \dfrac{k_1 + 1}{k_1 + 2} \\[4pt] y = \dfrac{k_2 + 1}{k_2 + 2} \\[4pt] y = \dfrac{3}{4x} \end{array} \right\}, \tag{8.7.2}$$

for $\frac{1}{2} < x < \frac{3}{4}$,
$$\left. \begin{array}{l} x = \dfrac{k_1 + 1}{2k_1 + 1} \\[4pt] y = \dfrac{k_2 + 1}{k_2 + 2} \\[4pt] y = \dfrac{4x}{3} \end{array} \right\}. \tag{8.7.3}$$

From (8.7.2), we obtain the following intervals for x:

$$\frac{4}{5} \quad \frac{5}{6} \quad \frac{6}{7} \quad \frac{7}{8} \quad \frac{9}{10} \quad \frac{15}{16}, \tag{8.7.4}$$

and from (8.7.3) the following ones:

$$\frac{3}{5} \quad \frac{2}{3}. \qquad (8.7.5)$$

A set of intervals composed from (8.7.1), (8.7.4), and (8.7.5) will be called *super-elite (3/4) intervals*.

As a result, we received the following set of intervals for Pelog:

super-elite (3/4) intervals	$\frac{1}{2}$	$\frac{3}{5}$	$\frac{2}{3}$	$\frac{3}{4}$	$\frac{4}{5}$	$\frac{5}{6}$	$\frac{6}{7}$	$\frac{7}{8}$	$\frac{9}{10}$	$\frac{15}{16}$	$\frac{1}{1}$
octave complements					$\frac{5}{8}$		$\frac{7}{12}$	$\frac{4}{7}$	$\frac{5}{9}$	$\frac{8}{15}$	

In this set, in addition to the super-elite (3/4) intervals, the octave complements, which are not the super-elite (3/4), are also shown. The Pelog system is given in Table 8.1.1.

8.8. Communicative Function of Elite Intervals

What is the function of projecting the subject's state which generates a musical interval? We put forth a hypothesis that this procedure performs a communicative function: the generation and perception of musical intervals make it possible to transfer of emotional states among individuals (see Lefebvre, 1990). The set of the subject's states (we will call them emotional states) is in one-to-one correspondence with the set of the values $R = D/s$.

Our hypothesis is as follows: *the musical interval is a code of the number R, that is, a code of the index of belief for the subject focused on the self.*

A general scheme of musical communication is shown on Fig.8.8.1.

Each state of a subject corresponds to a number R. From a 'technical' point of view, the transfer of the state consists of sending a signal (the physical agent) which carries an encoded state. In the perceptual system of the subject who receives the signal, an automatic process of decoding takes place, extracting information about R from the physical agent of its transferal. Then another automatic mechanism transfers the subject into the state corresponding to number R, that is, the state in which the sender of the signal has been. In this way emotions are passed from one subject to another.

If we accept this idea, then a musical interval is a special 'record' for a particular number. If not for its informational meaning it would be only 'noise', perceived by human auditory organs just as any other non-musical sound would be.

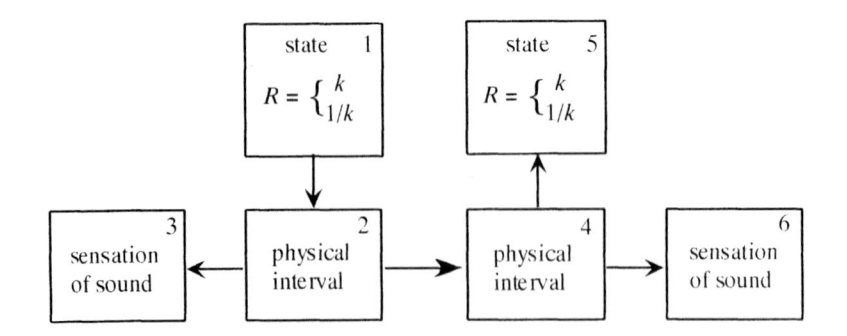

state 1: $R = \{{k \atop 1/k}\}$
state 5: $R = \{{k \atop 1/k}\}$
3 sensation of sound ← 2 physical interval ← state 1
state 1 → 2 physical interval → 4 physical interval → 6 sensation of sound
state 5 → 4 physical interval

Fig. 8.8.1. A scheme for transferal of an emotional state from a musician to a listener (Lefebvre, 1990).

Box 1 corresponds to the musician's emotional state characterized by a precise value R, where R is either a natural number or a number inverse to it. Box 2 corresponds to a projection of the emotional state onto a screen. This projection is a physical event consisting of two tones sounding either simultaneously or consecutively. Box 3 corresponds to the musician's perception of a sound merely as a physical irritant. Box 4 corresponds to the listener's perception of physical intervals. In this box, the processing of information goes in two ways. On the one hand, a received sound is transformed into a sensation of sound which by itself is not related to any emotional state. On the other hand, the precise value of R is extracted from a signal, and after that a special mechanism transfers the subject into an emotional state corresponding to R. Since all these processes run at the same time, we have the illusion that the sensation of sound is the reason for the appearance of an emotional state. In fact the emotional state is defined by the value R extracted from the signal, but not by the sensation of sound as a physical irritant.

Note that many researchers feel certain that the property of 'being musical' is a special acoustic peculiarity of a sound which creates a 'pleasant' feeling during its perception. Such ideas of musical sounds correspond to the lower row of boxes (Fig.8.8.1): a musician produces a sound, 'senses' it himself, and gives a listener the opportunity to 'sense' this sound, much in the way we sense weight, heat, or roughness. Without diminishing the importance of such acoustic properties as loudness and timbre, we nevertheless assume that the main factor which distinguishes a musical interval from any other pair of sounds is its informational content: its encoding of the number R.

The human perceptive mechanism does not need the exact values of elite intervals in order to transfer the number R. The only requirement is that the subject's perceptive system be able to restore this number unambiguously. Number R can be of two types: k or $1/k$. The states corresponding to them will be called of the first and the second type. States of the first type correspond to the values $x \geq 2/3$, and states of the second type to $x \leq 2/3$. (The state corresponding to $x = 2/3$ belongs to both types.) If the state of the first type is transferred, than a natural number k is expressed through x by the equation

$$k = \frac{2x - 1}{1 - x} \quad . \tag{8.8.1}$$

If the second type state is transferred, than k is expressed through x by the equation

$$k = \frac{1 - x}{2x - 1} \quad . \tag{8.8.2}$$

Equations (8.8.1) and (8.8.2) follow from equations (8.2.2) and (8.2.3) respectively. To extract information about a natural number, the subject's perceptive system must 'make computations' according to formulas (8.8.1) or (8.8.2).

The physical interval x^*, which carries the information about natural number k, may differ from the theoretical value of interval x corresponding to number k. Therefore, if we use value x^*, calculations with formulas (8.8.1) and (8.8.2) may give a rational number k^* different from k. Suppose that the subject's perceptive system chooses the natural number k closest to k^*. This assumption allows us to find the bounds of x^*'s deviations from x inside which k can be found unambiguously. When $x > 2/3$, the acceptable deviation can be found from inequality

$$\left| \frac{2x-1}{1-x} - \frac{2x^*-1}{1-x^*} \right| < \frac{1}{2}, \qquad (8.8.3)$$

and when $x < 2/3$ from inequality

$$\left| \frac{1-x}{2x-1} - \frac{1-x^*}{2x^*-1} \right| < \frac{1}{2}. \qquad (8.8.4)$$

Inequality (8.8.3) establishes the following bounds of deviation for x:

$$x - \frac{(1-x)^2}{1+x} < x^* < x + \frac{(1-x)^2}{3-x}, \qquad (8.8.5)$$

and inequality (8.8.4):

$$x - \frac{(2x-1)^2}{4x} < x^* < x + \frac{(2x-1)^2}{4(1-x)}. \qquad (8.8.6)$$

For the interval $x = 2/3$, the rightmost boundary is assigned by the right-hand part of (8.8.5), and the leftmost boundary is assigned by the left-hand part of (8.8.6):

$$2/3 - 1/24 < x^* < 2/3 + 1/21.$$

For the interval $x = 3/4$, the bounds are set by inequality (8.8.5):

$$3/4 - 1/28 < x^* < 3/4 + 1/36.$$

We can see that the tolerable deviations of x^* from x are much higher than those in European tempered tuning (see Table 8.1.1).

It seems that now we might find a reason for long and painful doubts in the Pythagorean hypothesis about the integer basis of musical intervals. The ideal proportions are indeed the ratios of integers, or, to be more precise, they are the ratios of the type

$$\frac{k+1}{k+2} \text{ and } \frac{k+1}{2k+1},$$

but they do not have to be realized precisely. We can even assume that Garbuzov's zones are the vicinities of the elite intervals corresponding to tolerable deviations. Expressions (8.8.5) and (8.8.6) allow us to calculate the exact bounds for these zones. Fig.8.8.2 represents a scale in cents, on which we have placed small circles corresponding to the exact values of elite intervals. The bounds of tolerable deviations are marked by *. In order to restore the precise ideal value of x based on a given empirical interval x^*, one has to plot x^* on a scale and find out into which elite interval's zone this value falls. This interval will be the precise theoretical value for a given interval x^*.

For example, let x_1^* be 360c. This interval belongs to the zone of the interval 4/5. Therefore, the theoretical value of x_1^* equivalent to 360c is 4/5. Let us note that the theoretical value of interval x_2^* equivalent to 420c is also 4/5. Thus, we can see that the two intervals which are equivalent from the informational point of view, differ by 60c. For the interval 2/3 the physical intervals that belong to its zone can differ by 228c, that is, by more than a tempered tone. From a psychoacoustic point of view, these two are completely different 'events'. But from the informational point of view, both intervals are codes for the same number $R = 1$.

We see that there is no theoretical basis for the assumption that in any given musical culture only intervals of certain fixed values can be used. Deviations from the ideal intervals may be dozens of times greater than in the tempered scale.

Proceeding from the same assumptions, we can find tolerable deviations from the ideal values for geometric proportions. The main inequality for geometric proportions (similar to the inequalities (8.8.3) and (8.8.4) in music) is

$$|k - k^*(x^*)| < 1/2 , \qquad (8.8.7.)$$

where k is a natural number corresponding to a given ideal proportion, x^* is the empirical value of a geometric proportion, and $k^*(x^*)$ is a value equal either to r

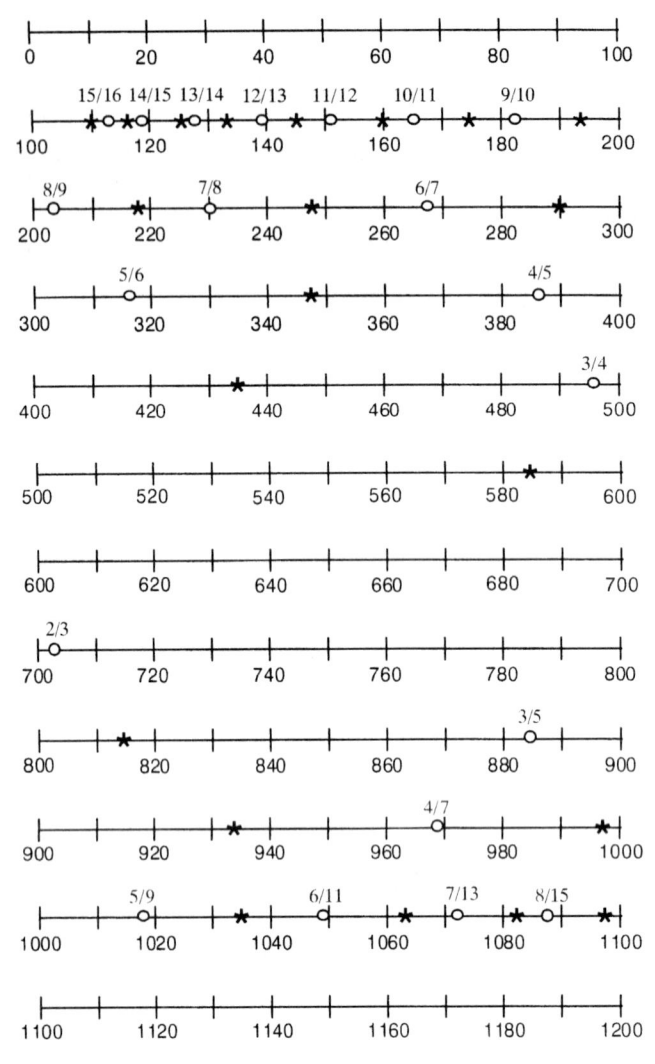

Fig. 8.8.2. A musical scale in cents, with elite intervals and Garbuzov's hypothetical zones marked on it.

On cent corresponds to 1/1200 of an octave measured on a logarithmic scale, that is, to the interval $(1/2)^{(1/1200)}$. Circles correspond to elite intervals, asterisks to the zone bounds. The zone limits were found with the help of our theoretical model of the subject.

or to $1/r$, where r can be found from equation (4.3.5) when $X_1 = x^*$: if $r \geq 1$, then $k^*(x^*) = r$, if $r < 1$, then $k^*(x^*) = 1/r$. The tolerable deviations from the golden section which were found with equation (8.8.7) are as follows:

$$(\frac{\sqrt{10}}{2} - 1) < x^* < \frac{2}{3} \quad \text{or} \quad 0.581 < x^* < 0.666. \tag{8.8.8}$$

We see that the difference between two empirical values, each of which represents the golden section, can reach 0.085. Apparently, this explains why attempts to empirically verify the special essence of the precise value of the golden section have always failed.

In actual psychological experiments, using inequality (8.8.7) we can hope to find verification of the special role of only those geometric proportions which correspond to the values of k equal to 1 and 2 in Table 4.3.1. The tolerable deviations for other ideal proportions are too small to be identified with experimental methods currently in use.

PART IX
THE SUBJECT WITH IMAGES OF SELF AND OTHER

9.1. An Abstract Scheme

As in section 1.1, assume that the subject lives in a world with two poles: one positive and one negative. In each situation, the world pushes the subject to choose one or the other pole. In addition to the initial subject, there is one other subject living in this world. The two subjects are always in one of two possible relationships with each other. We will call those relationships the first and the second. The subject has an image of the self, an image of the other, and an image of their relationship. In addition, the subject has an image of the group (consisting of himself and the other subject) as a separate unit, which can also be characterized by a particular degree of positivity.

Let us introduce the following variables:

u_1 is a measure of the world's pressure toward the positive pole
u_2 is a measure of the positivity of the subject's image of the self
u_3 is a measure of the positivity of the subject's image of the other
U_2 is a measure of the positivity of the subject's image of the group
U_1 is a measure of the subject's readiness to choose the positive pole

Variables $u_1, u_2, u_3, U_2,$ and U_1 are defined on the interval $[0,1]$. Analogously to our representation of the subject who has only an image of the self (see section 1.3), we will represent the subject with images of the self and other by the expression

$$U_1 = u_1^{U_2}. \tag{9.1.1}$$

For the case in which the subject has an image of the first relationship, let

$$U_2 = f_1(u_2, u_3), \tag{9.1.2}$$

where function $f_1(u_2,u_3)$ is such that with limit values of variables u_2 and u_3 (that is, when they are equal to either 1 or 0) the following equation holds

$$f_1(u_2, u_3) = \max(u_2, u_3), \tag{9.1.3}$$

i.e.,

$$f_1(1,1) = f_1(1,0) = f_1(0,1) = 1 \text{ and } f_1(0,0) = 0.$$

In the case, in which the subject has an image of the second relationship, let

$$U_2 = f_2(u_2, u_3), \tag{9.1.4}$$

such that with limit values of variables u_2 and u_3 the following equation holds:

$$f_2(u_2, u_3) = \min(u_2, u_3), \tag{9.1.5}$$

i.e.,

$$f_2(1,1) = 1, \text{ and } f_2(1,0) = f_2(0,1) = f_2(0,0) = 0.$$

Conditions (9.1.3) and (9.1.5) reflect the assumption that if, from the subject's point of view, both the subject and the other are ready to accomplish positive or negative action, then the measure of the group's positivity is equal to the measure of the positivity of the best of the two actions if the subject has an image of the first relationship, and equal to the measure of positivity of the worst of the two actions if he has an image of the second relationship.

9.2. Functions Corresponding to the Image of the Group

Assume that functions $f_1(u_2,u_3)$ and $f_2(u_2,u_3)$ are linear in relation to each of the variables u_2 and u_3. Thus they can be represented as bi-linear forms:

$$f_1(u_2, u_3) = a_0 + a_1 u_2 + a_2 u_3 + a_3 u_2 u_3, \tag{9.2.1}$$

$$f_2(u_2, u_3) = b_0 + b_1 u_2 + b_2 u_3 + b_3 u_2 u_3. \tag{9.2.2}$$

Coefficients for these forms can be found with the help of conditions (9.1.3) and (9.1.5). Therefore,

$$f_1(u_2, u_3) = u_2 + u_3 - u_2 u_3, \qquad (9.2.3)$$

$$f_2(u_2, u_3) = u_2 u_3. \qquad (9.2.4)$$

9.3. Analytical Representation of the Subject

Let us introduce a shortened version for the right hand side of equation (9.2.3):

$$u_2 \oplus u_3 =_{def} u_2 + u_3 - u_2 u_3.$$

Now variable U_2 can be represented with the two equations:

$$U_2 = u_2 \oplus u_3, \qquad (9.3.1)$$

$$U_2 = u_2 \bullet u_3. \qquad (9.3.2)$$

Equation (9.3.1) corresponds to the case in which the subject has an image of the first relationship, and equation (9.3.2) to the case in which the subject has an image of the second relationship. Let $X_1 = U_1$, $x_1 = u_1$, $X_2 = u_2$ and $Y_2 = u_3$. By using expressions (9.1.1), (9.3.1) and (9.3.2), we can represent the subject with the formula:

$$X_1 = x_1^{X_2 *_2 Y_2}, \qquad (9.3.3)$$

where $*_2 \in \{\oplus, \bullet\}$. Symbol $\oplus$ corresponds to an image of the first relationship, and symbol $\bullet$ to one of the second.

The same considerations for an image of the self result in

$$X_2 = x_2^{x_3 *_3 y_3}, \qquad (9.3.4)$$

where $X_2 = U_1$, $x_2 = u_1$, $x_3 = u_2$, $y_3 = u_3$, and $*_3 \in \{\oplus, \bullet\}$.

Substitute values from (9.3.4) for X_2 into (9.3.3) and obtain the final representation of the subject

$$X_1 = x_1^{x_2^{x_3 *_3 y_3} *_2 Y_2}. \qquad (9.3.5)$$

Suppose that the subject has a model of the group. We put it into correspondence with the expression $x_3 *_3 y_3$, where x_3, corresponds to the model of the self, y_3 to the model of the other, and $*_3$ to the model of their relationship.

9.4. The Principle of Maximization of the Ethical Status of the Image of the Self

Let us call the value of X_2 the ethical status of the image of the self (Lefebvre, 1980). Let values $*_2$ and $*_3$ be equal and let the subject which is described by (9.3.5) choose the value of the relationship 'by himself'. We can suppose that the value X_2 controls the subject's motivation during this choice: the subject chooses that value of $*_3$ which makes X_2 maximal. The following inequality holds:

$$x_2^{x_3 \bullet y_3} \geq x_2^{x_3 \oplus y_3}. \qquad (9.4.1)$$

Therefore, the first and second relationships are not equal. To maximize the ethical status of the image of the self, the subject would choose $\bullet$; in this case the subject looks better in his own eyes than if he chose relationship $\oplus$.

In the *Algebra of Conscience* (Lefebvre, 1982; enlarged edition 2001), a book in which inequality (9.4.1) plays a key role, it was shown that the interpretation of relationships $\oplus$ and $\bullet$ can be different in different cultures. In those cultures in which relationship $\bullet$ relates to compromise, people desiring to look better in their own eyes are willing to negotiate with each other. And in those cultures in which relationship $\bullet$ relates to conflict, people desiring to look better in their own eyes are uncompromising with each other.

PART X

THE ALGEBRAIC BASIS OF THE MODEL

10.1. Gamma-Algebra

In this part we will demonstrate that an abstract algebraic object which we call gamma-algebra underlies our model of the subject (Lefebvre, 1982). We introduce gamma-algebra as a set of three symbols:

$$<\Gamma, \rightarrow, |\ |>, \qquad (10.1.1)$$

where

Γ is a set with the power of continuum,

$\rightarrow$ is a binary operation which puts each pair $a, b \in \Gamma$ into correspondence with the only $c \in \Gamma$, i.e. $a \rightarrow b = c$, and

$|\ |$ is an operation 'norm' which establishes a one-to-one correspondence between the set Γ and the set of numbers from the interval [0,1], and for which the equation

$$|a \rightarrow b| = 1 - |a| + |a| \cdot |b|$$

holds.

The element $x \in \Gamma$, which is a solution of the equation $|x| = 1$, will be called 'one' and depicted **1**. The element $x \in \Gamma$, which is a solution of the equation $|x| = 0$, will be called 'zero' and depicted **0**. Let us now define a unary operation $\overline{}$ and the two binary operations $+$ and $\bullet$:

$$\overline{a} =_{def} a \rightarrow \mathbf{0}$$

$$a + b =_{def} (a \rightarrow \mathbf{0}) \rightarrow b = \overline{a} \rightarrow b$$

$$a \bullet b =_{def} (a \rightarrow (b \rightarrow \mathbf{0})) \rightarrow \mathbf{0} = \overline{\overline{a} + \overline{b}}$$

10.2. Axioms

To facilitate comparison of gamma-algebra with other algebraic objects we represent it as a redundant set of axioms.

I. Axioms of Equality

1. $a + b = b + a;\quad a \bullet b = b \bullet a$
2. $(a + b) + c = a + (b + c);\quad (a \bullet b) \bullet c = a \bullet (b \bullet c)$
3. $a + 0 = a;\quad a + 1 = 1$
4. $a \bullet 0 = 0;\quad a \bullet 1 = a$
5. $\overline{\overline{a}} = a$
6. $\overline{1} = 0;\quad \overline{0} = 1$
7. $\overline{a + b} = \overline{a} \bullet \overline{b};\quad \overline{a \bullet b} = \overline{a} + \overline{b}$
8. There exists a such that $a = \overline{a}$
9. $b \to a = \overline{b} + a$

II. Axioms of Order

1. For any a or b either $a \geq b$ or $b \geq a$
2. If $a \geq b$ and $b \geq c$, then $a \geq c$
3. If $a \geq b$ and $b \geq a$, then $a = b$
4. $1 \geq a;\quad a \geq 0$

III. Axioms Connecting Binary Operations + and • and Order

1. $a + b \geq a,\quad a \geq a \bullet b$
2. If $a \geq b$, then $c + a \geq c + b$ and $c \bullet a \geq c \bullet b$
3. If $a \geq b$, then equations $a \bullet x = b$ and $b + x = a$ have solutions

4. If $a \geq b$, where $a \neq 1$ and $b \neq 0$, then there exist natural numbers N_1 and N_2 such that $b \geq a^{N_1}$ and $N_2 b \geq a$, where

$$a^{N_1} = \underbrace{a \cdot a \cdot \ldots \cdot a}_{N_1 \text{ times}} \text{ and } N_2 b = \underbrace{b + b + \ldots + b}_{N_2 \text{ times}}.$$

IV. Axiom Connecting the Unary Operation and Order

1. If $a \geq b$, then $\overline{b} \geq \overline{a}$.

10.3. Algebraic Subject

Let us agree to write a^b instead of $b \to a$. Now we can have a new view of our model. The subject which has only an image of the self corresponds to equation

$$X_1 = x_1^{x_2^{x_3}}. \tag{10.3.1}$$

Expression (10.3.1) corresponds to the following expression from gamma-algebra

$$A_1 = a_1^{a_2^{a_3}}, \tag{10.3.2}$$

where

a_1 is a root of equation $|x| = x_1$;
a_2 is a root of equation $|x| = x_2$;
a_3 is a root of equation $|x| = x_3$;
A_1 is a root of equation $|x| = X_1$;

A subject which, in addition to the image of the self, also has an image of the other corresponds to the expression

$$X_1 = x_1^{X_2 *_2 Y_2}, \tag{10.3.3}$$

where $*_2 \in \{\oplus, \bullet\}$.

Expression (10.3.3) corresponds to the following expression from gamma-algebra:

$$A_1 = a_1^{A_2 \otimes_2 B_2}, \qquad (10.3.4)$$

where $\otimes \in \{+, \bullet\}$. Values A_1, a_1, A_2, and B_2 are the roots of equations $|x| = X_1$, $|x| = x_1$, $|x| = X_2$, and $|x| = Y_2$, respectively. Arithmetic operation $\oplus$ corresponds to operation $+$ from gamma-algebra, and arithmetic operation $\bullet$ to gamma-algebra operation $\bullet$. What is the difference between expressions (10.3.1) and (10.3.3), on the one hand, and expressions (10.3.2) and (10.3.4), on the other? The former are numerical functions describing the subject. The latter are theoretical analogues of the subject as such. The elements of gamma-algebra are theoretical analogues of the subject's states, and operations $+$ and $\bullet$ are theoretical analogues of the relationships between subjects.

CONCLUSION

This model is a hypothesis. It predicts certain things, and if its predictions are not verified the model must be rejected. In what follows we describe three experiments which can be considered the first step in testing this model.

The first experiment will answer the question of whether the model is suitable for a case in which the subject makes his decision based on perceptual information about the object (see section 3.1).

The experimental material consists of several sets of stimuli having sensory magnitude such as length, duration, loudness, weight, etc. Each set contains stimuli evenly distributed on a psychological scale (magnitude scale). One group of subjects works with one set of stimuli only. In the beginning of the experiment the subjects are presented with the stimuli of maximum and minimum magnitude. After that they are asked to estimate the magnitude of each stimulus with reference to a scale with k labels, where label 1 corresponds to the stimulus with the weakest magnitude, and k to the one with the strongest (k=7 to 11). The mean value for each stimulus is calculated based on this experiment. The description of the methods for conducting these experiments is given in Stevens & Galanter (1957).

Conjecture 1.

For stimuli evenly distributed on a psychological scale the following rational law holds:

$$x = \frac{2x_1}{1+x_1},$$

where x *is a normalized evaluation of the stimulus on the scale* 1, 2, ..., k *and* x_1 *is the normalized psychological magnitude of the same stimulus (see details in section 3.2). We expect graphs constructed according to these experimental data to have the* shape indicated in Fig.3.2.4 (for $x_2 = 0.5$).

The second experiment will answer the question of whether the model is suitable for a case in which the subject makes his decision not based on perceptual information about an object on which his activity is focused (see section 5.1).

Each subject must evaluate the degree of 'lightness' of a rectangle (reflection 19%) located between a dark one (reflection 5%) and a light one (reflection 83%). The evaluation is performed on a 100-point scale, where 0 corresponds to the dark rectangle and 100 to the light one. Each subject makes only one mark on the scale. A curve of the density of evaluation is constructed based on the data (see details in Poulton & Simmonds, 1985). The subjective lightness of the rectangle with reflection 19% is close to the midpoint between black and white. Therefore, one could expect a peak of density near point 50. But the data provided by Poulton & Simmonds (1985) suggest that the subjects escape the middle mark and shift from it to the right or to the left. The model proposed by us explains this phenomenon (see section 5.4). In addition, the model predicts the points of the two peaks. (The data by Poulton & Simmonds are not sufficient to verify this.)

Conjecture 2.

The peaks of density on a 100-point scale will appear at the dots 37.2 and 61.8 (see Fig.5.4.1). The model passes the test if the two experimental peaks together with their intervals of confidence are located inside the intervals [33.4, 41.9] and [58.1, 66.6] respectively (see expression 8.8.8).

The third experiment concerns our presumption that the same subject's state, characterized by number X, can reveal itself both as a ratio of two physical values equal to X and as a probability equal to X (see Section 2.2).

The material for this experiment is ten to twelve Chinese-like characters; the subjects must not know the Chinese language at all. The experiment consists of two phases. During the first phase the subjects are presented with the Chinese-like characters one by one. Each character is presented several times. There must be five to six different numbers of time of presentation, and maximal number must be a few times greater than the number preceding it.

The second phase is conducted with the same subjects. They are told that the characters they have been shown stand for adjectives and asked to guess their meaning on the good-bad scale (the details are described in Zajonc, 1968).

The subjects are divided into two groups. The first group makes its evaluation on the scale 0, 1, 2, ..., k, where 0 corresponds to 'bad' and k to 'good' (k is equal to 6-11). Then we have to calculate the mean evaluation s of those characters which were presented the greatest number of times in the first phase.

The second group uses a binary scale 0, 1 (0 stands for 'bad', and 1 for 'good'). Then we have to find the frequency p of a positive evaluation of those characters which were presented the greatest number of times in the first phase. Each subject in this group evaluates each character only once.

Conjecture 3.

$$\frac{s}{k} = p = 0.618.$$

The model passes the test if the values found in the experiment for both s/k and p, together with their intervals of confidence, are located inside the interval [0.581, 0,666] (see expression 8.8.8).

A new material added to section 5.5 supports Conjecture 3: in estimation an object presented earlier on scale 0-6, the mean value is equal to 0.63 of the scale length, and bipolar evaluation it is ≈ 0.62.

REFERENCES

Adams-Webber, J. *Personal Construct Theory: Concepts and Applications*. New York: Willey, 1979.

_____. Assimilation and Contrast in Personal Judgment. In: Mancuso, J.C. & Adams-Webber, J. (Eds.), *The Construing Person*, New York: Praeger, 1982.

_____. Self-Other Contrast and the Development of Personal Construct. *Canadian Journal of the Behavioral Sciences*, **17**, 303-314, 1985a.

_____. Construing Self and Others. In: Epting, F.R. & Landfield, A.W. (Eds.), *Anticipating Personal Construct Psychology*. Lincoln: University of Nebraska Press, 1985b.

Adams-Webber, J. & Benjafield, J. The Relation between Lexical Marking and Rating Extremity in Interpersonal Judgment. *Canadian Journal of Behavioral Sciences*, **5**, 234-241, 1973.

Adams-Webber, J. & Rodney, Y. Rational Aspects of Temporary Changes in Construing Self and Others. *Canadian Journal of Behavioral Sciences*, **15**, 52-59, 1983.

Anderson, N. H. *Foundations of Information Integration Theory*. New York: Academic Press, 1981.

Archibald, R. C. Notes on the Logarithmic Spiral, Golden Section, and the Fibonacci Series. In: Hambidge, J. *Dynamic Symmetry in the Greek Vase*. New Haven: Yale University Press, 1920.

Balzano, G. J. The Group-Theoretic Description of 12-fold and Microtonal Pitch System. *Computer Music Journal*, **4**, 66-84, 1980.

Barnett, J. D. *The Operation of the Initiative, Referendum and Recall in Oregon*. New York: The Macmillan Co., 1915.

Benjafield, J. On the Relations between Pollyana and Golden Section Hypotheses. *British Journal of Social Psychology*, **23**, 83-84, 1984.

_____. A Review of Recent Research on the Golden Section. *Empirical Studies of the Art*, **3**(8), 117-134, 1985.

Benjafield J. & Adams-Webber, J. The Golden Section Hypothesis. *British Journal of Psychology*, **67**, 11-15, 1976.

Benjafield, J. & Green, T.R.G. Golden Section Relations in Interpersonal Judgment. *British Journal of Psychology*, **69**, 25-35, 1978.

Benjafield, J., Pomeroy, E., & Saunders, M.A. The Golden Section and the Accuracy with which Proportions Are Drawn. *Canadian Journal of Psychology / Review Canadian Psychology*, **34**(3), 253-256, 1980.

Berlyne, D. E. *Aesthetics and Psychobiology*. New York: Appleton-Century-Crofts, 1971.

Berscheid, E. & Walster, E. When Does a Harm-Doer Compensate a Victim? *Journal of Personality and Social Psychology*, **6**, 435-441, 1967.

Bigava, Z. 1. A Character of Setting Effects in Various Moving Problems. In: Nadirashvili, S. A., *Voprosy Inzhenernoy i Socialnoy Psichologii*, **II**, Tbilisi: Metsniereba, 1979.

Birnbaum, M. H. Controversies in Psychophysical Measurement. In: Wegener, B. (Ed.), *Social Attitudes and Psychophysical Measurement*. Hillside, NJ: Lawrence Erlbaum Associates, 1982.

Bonnano, G. A. & Stillings, N. A. Preference, Familiarity, and Recognition after Repeated Brief Exposure to Random Geometric Shapes. *American Journal of Psychology*, **99**, 3, 403-415, 1986.

Brock, T. C. & Becker, L. A. "Debriefing" and Susceptibility to Subsequent Experimental Manipulations. *Journal of Personality and Social Psychology*, **2**, 314-323, 1966.

Burns, E. M. & Ward, W. D. Intervals, Scales, and Tuning. In: Deutsch, D. (Ed.), *The Psychology of Music*. New York: Academic Press, 1982.

Butler, D. & Ranney, A. *Referendums*. Washington, D.C.: American Enterprise Institute for Public Policy Research, 1978.

Carlsmith, J.M. & Gross, A. Some Effects of Guilt on Compliance. *Journal of Personality and Social Psychology*, **11**, 240-244, 1969.

Carlson, M. & Miller, N. Explanation of the Relation between Negative Mood and Helping. *Psychological Bulletin*, **102**, 91-108, 1987.

Chavchanidze, V. V. Setting Theory of Decision Making and Automated Mechanisms of Human Behavior. In: Zhukovin, V. E. (Ed.), *Priniatie Resheniia Chelovekom*, Proceedings for the Third Symposium on Cybernetics, 1967.

Cohen, H. F. *Quantifying Music*. Dordrecht, Holland: D. Reidel, 1984.

Colman, S. & Coan, C. A. *Proportional Form*. New York: G. P. Putnam's Sons, 1920.

Darlington, R. B. & Macker, C. E. Displacement of Guilt-Produced Altruistic Behavior. *Journal of Personality and Social Behavior*, **4**, 442-443, 1966.

Davis, F. C. Aesthetic Proportion. *American Journal of Psychology*, **45**, 298-302, 1933.

Davis, S. T. & Jahnke, J. C. Unity and the Golden Section: Rules for Aesthetic Choice? *American Journal of Psychology*, **104**, 2, 257-277, 1991.

Doczi, G. *The Power of Limits*. Boulder: Shambhala, 1981.

Dowling, W. J. & Harwood, D. L. *Music Cognition*. Orlando: Academic Press, 1986.

Elfner, L. Systematic Shifts in the Judgment of Octaves of High Frequencies. *Journal of the Acoustical Society of America*, **36**, 270-276, 1964.

Eu, M. F. *Statement of Vote*. Sacramento, 1983a,b, 1985a,b, 1987, 1989a,b,c.

Fechner, G. T. Vorschule der Aesthetik (Introduction to Aesthetics). Berlin. 1876.

Feynman, R. P. Leichton, R. B., & Sands, M. *The Feynman Lectures on Physics*. Reading: Addison-Wesley, 1966.

Freedman, J. L., Wallington, S. S., & Bless, E. Compliance without Pressure: The Effect of Guilt. *Journal of Personality and Social Psychology*, **7**, 117-124, 1967.

Garbuzov, N. A. *Zonnaya Priroda Zvukovysotnogo Slukha* (Zone Nature of Pitch Hearing). Moscow: Institute of Psychology Press, 1948.

_____. Excerpts from the books Zone Nature of Pitch Hearing and Zone Nature of Tempo and Rhythm. *Psichologicheskii Zhurnal*, **11**, 3, 149-156, 1990.

Ghyka, M. C. *The Geometry of Art and Life*. New York: Sheed and Ward, 1946.

Glover, J. *Responsibility*. New York: Humanities Press, 1970.

Godkewitsch, M. The "Golden Section": An Artifact of Stimulus Range and Measure of Preference. *American Journal of Psychology*, **87**, 269-277, 1974.

Grice, J. W., McDaniel, B. L., Thompsen, D. Testing an Algebraic Model of Self-Reflexion. *Perceptual and Motor Skills*, **100**, 1036-1048, 2005.

Hambidge, J. *Dynamic Symmetry in the Greek Vase*. New Haven, Connecticut: Yale University Press, 1920.

Harrison, A. A. Mere Exposure. *Advances in Experimental Social Psychology*, **10**, 39-83, 1977.

Helmholtz, H. L. F. *On the Sensations of Tone as a Physiological Basis for the Theory of Music*. English translations (1954). New York: Dover Publications, Inc., 1877.

Helson, H. Adaptation Level as Frame of Reference for Prediction of Psychological Data. *American Journal of Psychology*, **60**, 1-29, 1947.

_____. *Adaptation-Level Theory*. New York: Harper & Row, 1964.

Jastrow, J. The Psychophysic Law and Star Magnitude. *American Journal of Psychology*, **1**, 112-127, 1887.

Kelly, G. A. *The Psychology of Personal Constructs*. New York: Norton, 1955.

Kenny, A. Free *Will and Responsibility*. London: Routledge & Kegan Paul, 1978.

Krueger, F. Die Theorie der Konsonans. *Psychol. Studien*, **5**, 294-409, 1910.

Krueger, L. E. Reconciling Fechner and Stevens: Toward a Unified Psychophysical Law. *Behavioral and Brain Sciences*, **12**, 251-320, 1989.

Krumhansl, C. L. *Cognitive Foundations of Musical Pitch*. New York: Oxford University Press, 1990.

Krumhansl, C. L. & Jusczyk, P.W. Infant's Perception of Phrase Structure in Music. *Psychological Science*, **1**, 1-4, 1990.

Krumhansl, C. L. & Kessler, E. J. Tracing the Dynamic Changes in Perceived Tonal Organization in a Spatial Representation of Musical Keys. *Psychological Review*, **89**, 334-68, 1982.

Krumhansl, C. L. & Shepard, R. N. Quantification of the Hierarchy of Tonal Functions within a Diatonic Context. *Journal of Experimental Psychology: Human Perception & Performance*, **5**, 579-594, 1979.

Kunst, J. *Music in Java*, Vol. I & II. Martinus Nijhoff, 1949.

Kunst-Wilson, W. R. & Zajonc, R. B. Affective Discrimination of Stimuli that Cannot Be Recognized. *Science*, **207**, 557-558, 1980.

Lalo, C. *L'esthetique Experimentale Contemporaine*. Paris: Alcan, 1908.

Le Corbusier. *The Modular*. Cambridge, Mass.: MIT Press, 1968.

Lefebvre, V. A. Basic Ideas of the Logic of Reflexive Games. In: *Problemy Issledovaniia Sistem i Struktur*. Moscow: Academy of Sciences of the USSR Press, 1965.

_____. *Konfliktuiushchie Struktury* (Conflicting Structures). Moscow: Vysshaya Shkola, 1967.

_____. A Formal Method of Investigating Reflective Processes. *General Systems*, **17**, 181-188, 1972.

_____. *The Structure of Awareness: Toward a Symbolic Language of Human Reflexion*. Beverly Hills: Sage Publications, 1977.

_____. An Algebraic Model of Ethical Cognition. *Journal of Mathematical Psychology*, **22**, 83-120, 1980.

_____. *Algebra of Conscience: A Comparative Analysis of Western an Soviet Ethical Systems*. Dordrecht, Holland: Reidel, 1982.

_____. The Principle of Complementarity As the Basis for the Model of Ethical Cognition. *Journal of Social and Biological Structures*, **7**, 243-258, 1984.

_____. The Golden Section and an Algebraic Model of Ethical Cognition.. *Journal of Mathematical Psychology*, **29**, 289-310, 1985.

_____. The Fundamental Structures of Human Reflexion. *Journal of Social and Biological Structures*, **10**, 129-175, 1987a.

_____. Response to McClain. *Journal of Social and Biological Structures*, **10**, 236-237, 1987b.

_____. McClain Circle and Plato's Harp. *Journal of Social and Biological Structures*, **12**, 73-81, 1989.

_____. The Fundamental Structures of Human reflexion (revised). In: Wheeler, H. (Ed.), *The Structure of Human Reflexion: The Reflexional Psychology of Vladimir Lefebvre*. New York: Peter Lang, 1990.

_____. A Rational Equation for Attractive Proportions. *Journal of Mathematical Psychology*, **36**, 100-128, 1992.

_____. *Algebra of Conscience*, second enlarged edition. Kluwer Academic Publishers, 2001.

Lefebvre, V. A. & Garfias, R. On the Nature of Musical Intervals, (unpublished manuscript), 1991.

Lefebvre, V. A., Lefebvre, V. D., & Adams-Webber, J. Modeling an Experiment on Construing Self and Others. *Journal of Mathematical Psychology*, **30**, 317-330, 1986.

Lefebvre, V. D. Choice Without Criteria of Preference. In: Wheeler, H. (Ed.), *The Structure of Human Reflexion: The Reflexional Psychology of Vladimir Lefebvre*. New York: Peter Lang, 1990.

Lerner, M. J. The effect of Responsibility and Choice on a Partner's Attractiveness Following Failure. *Journal of Personality*, **33**, 178-187, 1965.

Lerner, M. J. & Matthews, G. Reactions to Suffering of Others under Conditions of Indirect Responsibility. *Journal of Personality and Social Psychology*, **5**, 319-325, 1967.

Lipps, Th. *Psychologishe Studien*. Leipzig: Durr'sche Buchhandlung, 1905.

Lockhead, G. R. Category Bounds and Stimulus Variability. In: Shepp, B.E. & Ballesteros, S. (Eds.), *Object Perception*, Hillside, N.J.: Lawrence Erlbaum Associates, 1989.

Losskii, N. *Svoboda Voli* (Free Will), Paris: YMCA Press, 1927.

Lynch, M. P., Eilers, R. E., Oller, D. R., & Urbano, R. C. Innateness, Experience, and Music Perception. *Psychological Science*, **1**, 272-276, 1991.

Mandler, G., Nakamura, Y., & VanZandt, B. J. S. Nonspecific Effects of Exposure on Stimuli that Cannot Be Recognized. *Journal of Experimental Psychology: Learning, Memory, and Cognition*, **13**, 646-648, 1987.

Marczewska, H. Golden Section or Lack of Symmetry. *Polish Psychological Bulletin*, **14**, 85-91, 1983.

Marks, L. E. Stimulus Range, Number of Categories, and Form of the Category-Scale. *American Journal of Psychology*, **81**, 467-79, 1968.

McClain, E. *The Pythagorean Plato*. Stony Brook: Nicolas Hays, 1976.

_____. Comment on Vladimir Lefebvre's Tonal Automata. *Journal of Social and Biological Structures*, **10**, 204-212, 1987.

McGraw, K. M. Subjective Probabilities and Moral Judgments. *Journal of Experimental and Social Psychology*, **14**, 501-518, 1985.

Messick, D. M. Egocentric Biases and the Golden Section. *Journal of Social and Biological Structures*, **10**, 241-247, 1987.

Meyer, M. F. Listeners Can Be Seduced to Perceive the Paradoxical Ratio 51:87 as either One or Another Truly Melodical Interval. *The Journal of the Acoustical Society of America*, **4**, 1277, 1962a.

_____. Helmholtz's Aversion to Tempered Tuning Experimentally Shown to Be a Neurological Problem. *The Journal of the Acoustical Society of America*, **34**, 127-128, 1962b.

Orlov, Yu. F. A Quantum Model of Doubt. *Annals of the New York Academy of Sciences*, **373**, 84-92, 1981.

Osgood, C. E,, Suci, G. J. & Tannenbaum, P. H. *The Measurement of Meaning*. Urbana: University of Illinois Press, 1957.

Oshins, E. & McGoveran, D. Thoughts about Logic about Thoughts...: The Question of Schizophrenia. In: Banathy, B. (Ed.), *Systems Science and Science* (Proceedings of Symposium "Psychotherapy, Mind, and Brain"), 1980.

Parducci, A. Direction of Shift in the Judgment of Single Stimuli. *Journal of Experimental Psychology*, **51**, 169-178, 1956.

_____. Category Judgment: A Range-Frequency Model. *Psychological Review*, **72**, 407-418, 1965.

Piehl, J. The "Golden Section": An Artifact of Stimulus Range and Demand Characteristics. *Perceptual and Motor Skills*, **43**, 47-50, 1976.

Plomp, R. & Levelt, W. J. M. Tonal Consonance and Critical Bandwidth. *The Journal of Acoustical Society of America*, **38**, 548-560, 1965.

Plug, C. The Golden Section Hypothesis. *American Journal of Psychology*, **93**, 467-487, 1980.

Poulton, E. C. *Bias in Quantifying Judgments*. Hove & London: Lawrence Erlbaum, 1989.

Poulton, E. S. & Simmonds, D. C. V. Subjective Zeros, Subjectively Equal Stimulus Spacing, and Contraction Biases in Very First Judgments of Lightness. *Perception & Psychophysics*, **37**, 420-428, 1985.

Poulton E. C., Simmonds, D. C. V., & Warren, R. M. Response Bias in Very First Judgments of the Reflectance of Grays: Numerical versus Linear Estimates. *Perception and Psychophysics*, **3**, 112-114, 1968.

Ranney, A. The Year of the Referendum. *Public Opinion*, **1**, No.5, 26-28, 1978.

_____. Referendums, 1980 Style. *Public Opinion*, **4**, No.1, 40-44, 1981.

_____. The Year of the Referendum. *Public Opinion*, **5**, No.6, 12-14, 1983.

_____. Referendums and Initiatives 1984. *Public Opinion*, **7**, No.6, 15-17, 1985.

_____. Referendums and Initiatives 1986. *Public Opinion*, **9**, No.5, 44-46, 1987.

_____. Election '88. Referendums. *Public Opinion*, **11**, No.5, 15-17, 1989.

Regan, J. W. Guilt, Perceived Injustice, and Altruistic Behavior. *Journal of Personality and Social Psychology*, **18**, No.1, 124-132, 1971.

Reznik, V. 1. A Sensory Stage of Perception of One's Own Inner Feelings. In: Banshchikov, V. M. (Ed.), *Problemy Lichnosti*. Materialy Simpoziuma, Moscow, 1969.

Rigdon, M. A. & Epting, F. A Test of the Golden Section Hypothesis with Elicited Constructs. *Journal of Personality and Social Psychology*, **43**, 1080-1087, 1982.

Romany, S. & Adams-Webber, J. The Golden Section Hypothesis from a Developmental Perspective. *Social Behavior and Personality*, **9**, 89-92, 1981.

Schiffman, H. R. & Bobko, D. J. Preference in Linear Partitioning: The Golden Section Re-Examined. *Perception and Psychophysics*, **24**, 102-103, 1978.

Schwartz, R. M. & Garamoni, G. L. A Structural Model of Positive and Negative States of Mind: Asymmetry in the Internal Dialogue. In: P. C. Kendall

(Ed.), *Advances in Cognitive Behavioral Research and Therapy*, (Vol.5, pp.1-62). New York: Academic Press, 1986.

Schwartz, R. M. & Michelson, L. States of the Mind Model: Cognitive Balance in the Treatment of Agoraphobia. *Journal of Consulting and Clinical Psychology*, **55**, 557-565, 1987.

Seamon, J. G., Brody, N., & Kauff, D. M. Affective Discrimination of Stimuli that Are Not Recognized: Effects of Shadowing, Masking, and Cerebral Laterality. *Journal of Experimental Psychology: Learning, Memory, and Cognition*, **9**, 544-555, 1983.

Shepard, R. N. Geometrical Approximation to the Structure of Musical Pitch. *Psychological Review*, **89**, 305-333, 1982a.

____. Structural Representation of Musical Pitch. In: Deutsch, D. (Ed.), *The Psychology of Music*, New York: Academic Press, 1982b.

Shipley, W. C., Daltman, P. E., & Steele, B. A. The Influence of Size on Preference for Rectangular Proportion in Children and Adults. *Journal of Experimental Psychology*, **37**, 333-336, 1947.

Simmons, C. H. & Lerner, M. J. Altruism as a Search for Justice. *Journal of Personality and Social Psychology*, **9**, 216-225, 1968.

Stevens, S. S. A Scale for the Measurement of a Psychological Magnitude: Loudness. *Psychological Review*, **43**, 405-416, 1936.

Stevens, S. S. *Psychophysics*, New York: John Wiley & Sons, 1975.

Stevens, S. S. & Galanter, E. H. Ratio Scales and Category Scales for a Dozen Perceptual Continua. *Journal of Experimental Psychology*, **54**, 377-411, 1957.

Stumpf, C. *Tonpsychologie*, 2 vols., Leipzig: S. Hirzel, 1883-90.

Svensson, L. T. Note on the Golden Section. *Scandinavian Journal of Psychology*, **18**, 79-80, 1977.

Terhardt, E. Pitch, Consonance, and Harmony. *Journal of Acoustical Society of America*, **55**, 1061-1069, 1974.

Thompson, G. G. The Effect of Chronologic Age on Aesthetic Preference for Rectangles of Different Proportions. *Journal of Experimental Psychology*, **36**, 50-58, 1946.

Trehub, S. E. Infants' Perception of Musical Patterns. *Perception and Psychophysics*, **41**, 6, 635-641, 1987.

Tuohy, A. P. Affective Asymmetry in Social Perception. *British Journal of Psychology*, **78**, 41-51, 1987.

Tuohy, A. P. & Stradling, S. G. Maximum Salience vs. Golden Section Proportions in Judgmental Asymmetry. *British Journal of Psychology*, **78**, 457-464, 1987.

Tversky, A. & Kahneman, D. The Framing of Decisions and the Psychology of Choice. *Science*, **211**, 453-458, 1981.

Valentine, C. W. *The Experimental Psychology of Beauty*. London: Methuen & Co. Ltd., 1962.

Wallace, J. & Sadalla, E. Behavioral Consequences of Transgression: 1. The Effect of Social Recognition. *Journal of Experimental Research in Personality*, **1**, 187-194, 1966.

Ward, W. D. Subjective Musical Pitch. *Journal of the Acoustical Society of America*, **26**, 369-380, 1954.

_____. On the Perception of the Frequency Ratio 55:32. *Journal of the Acoustical Society of America*, **34**, 679, 1962.

Ward, W. D. & Martin, D. W. Psychophysical Comparison of Just Tuning and Equal Temperament in Sequences of Individual Tones. *Journal of the Acoustical Society of America*, **33**, 586-588, 1961.

Zajonc, R. B. Attitudinal Effects of Mere Exposure. *Journal of Personality and Social Psychology. Monograph Supplement*, **9**, No.2, Part 2, 1-32, 1968.

POST SCRIPT

Text written by Sir Karl Popper.*

Sir Karl Popper suggested that I begin this book with the following words of his own composition:

I think I made a strong psychological discovery.

It consists of several stages. It is an oversimplification. It belongs, in a new sense, to moral psychology.

I suggest that there are two influences in our minds which influence our readiness to act well:

(a) Pressure from the outside world (State of Society, State of Nature, the money I have...)

(b) Our own idea of the outside world, summed up in a simple judgment: how good or how bad is it.

These two influences act upon our otherwise independent (good or bad) intuitions.

As you see, this contains a colossal simplification: that such polarity as good-bad, plays a decisive role in our moral actions. No psychologist will like this. Everyone will say that this means thinking of man as an essentially moral being.

Let us leave all this for the moment. Wait and see what my analysis can explain.

---

* Published by permission of Sir Karl Popper.

The Additional Part
Bipolar Choice

Introduction

Mentalism is a science about subjective matters that gives a living creature a niche for the inner world. Behaviorism is a science about behavior depriving a living creature of it. Both of these sciences have a common feature: an organism appears as an entity in them. The first one focuses on a subject's relation to the self, while the second one focuses on the relations between the subject and the environment. For the last few decades, the border between mentalism and behaviorism has moved: a formal model of the subject has appeared which includes both its mental domain and its interrelation with the environment. The model's verification goes through its penetration into various branches of psychology, sociology, and anthropology. Behaviorism represents the most attractive field for such penetration, because of its strict inner discipline and methodological honesty that allows us to distinguish clearly what is understood and what is not. One of the unsolved problems in the science of behavior is the *Matching Law* (Herrnstein, 1961). It describes the ability of birds and mammals to regulate the ratio between a sequence of reinforcements and a sequence of responses. This ability looks *strange* from the point of view of the utilitarian common sense (see Williams, 1988).

In this Part we offer a solution to this problem with the help of the model of *the subject with internality*, MS (introduced in section 4 of this Part). The model is based on the assumption that the subject's actions depend not only on external influences but also on the internal variable which is capable of changing independently from the external influences. There are clear parallels between MS and the model described in the main text of the book, Intentional Model, although the two models are constructed on different bases. MS enriches the Intentional Model, because it connects variable x_2 (which represents an image of the external world in the Intentional Model) with the internal variable S (which shows the ability of an organism to withstand the pressure of the environment).

In creating MS, we tried to understand a phenomenon of 'moral choice' from a purely scientific point of view, rather than from a moralistic one. A great number of specialists from psychiatrists to sociologists studying criminals and terrorists are interested in finding objective laws of moral choice. MS reflects two aspects of the subject's activity: utilitarian and deontological. The utilitarian aspect relates to the behavior which is advantageous from the practical point of view, for example, obtaining money or food. The deontological aspect relates to the idealistic behavior, for example, choosing between 'good' and 'evil'. It may happen that the 'moral' orientation of the alternative does not correspond to the utilitarian one. For example, a deal with an enemy may be more profitable than a treaty with a friend. Both these aspects are connected into a single process of behavior generation by the formal model.

MS is a probabilistic model. It predicts probabilities with which the subject chooses the alternatives, one playing the role of the positive pole and the other that of the negative pole. The idea that the subject's choice is probabilistic appeared early in the twentieth century and was used in many theoretical models (Thurstone, 1927; von Neuman & Morgenstern, 1944; Savage, 1951; Mosteller & Nogee, 1951; Bradley & Terry, 1952; Davidson, Suppes & Siegel, 1957; Bower, 1959; Luce, 1959; Audley, 1960; Spence, 1960; Restle, 1961; LaBerge, 1962; Atkinson et al., 1965). This line of investigations has significantly changed the view on behavior being a process completely determined by the environment. Although effective methods have been developed to predict the results of probabilistic choice, a problem of its essence remained untouched. We still do not have clear ideas about whether all living creatures are capable of probabilistic choice or only some of them. We do not know either how an organism 'learns' the probabilities with which it 'must' make a choice in a given situation. MS connects the subject's probabilistic behavior with its mental domain and allows us to formulate a few new hypotheses. We assume that in the framework of this model, prior to the act of choice, the subject's state is uncertain and can be characterized by the distribution of probabilities of alternative choices. If we use a metaphor from the quantum mechanic, we would say that immediately before the act of choice, the subject is in a mixed state, and the act of choice is a 'collapse' of the mixed state. As a result, the subject moves into one of the pure states. It is important to emphasize that the subject's ability to make a choice between the alternatives with *fixed* probabilities indicates a rather high level of the development. The specialists in mathematical modeling know well how difficult it is to construct a technical device which would generate a random sequence of zeros and ones with a fixed probability of their appearance. It is possible that the organism's ability to give response undetermined by a stimulus raises its chances to find food and not to become another organism's food (Lefebvre, 1999).

We may suppose that in evolution, probabilistic behavior of organisms appears at the same time as their mental domain. Their appearance indicates the moment of an organism's 'liberation' from the 'necessity' to respond in one only way to an external influence. To choose alternatives with fixed probabilities, the organism must somehow 'download' them into the self. We presume that the 'secret' of the Matching Law is that it reflects a procedure of forming a mixed state in the subject, during which the subject processes information received from the environment into a probabilistic distribution. Let us imagine that an organism, say of a rat, a pigeon, and even a man, cannot solve this problem through their inner mental activity. Because of that, the entire organism becomes involved in a computational process. When an animal is running between the two food-hoppers (in the experiments in which the Matching Law is revealed), it is an external demonstration of this process, whose goal is to generate *frequencies* which would later transform into *probabilities*. As a result of such 'downloading' of the probability, the subject became capable of making an instant probabilistic choice. But this ability is not 'free' for the subject; to obtain it an organism must spend energy.

The experiments with two keys in which human subjects were used (see Ruddle et al., 1979; Wearden & Burgess, 1982) allow us to hypothesize that generation of a mixed state in humans is also connected with their motor activity, which may also reveal itself during a process of estimation. For example, when the subject is given a task to mark the intensity of a stimulus on a scale, the subject's pencil oscillates before it makes the final mark. Sometimes it is even difficult to determine which mark is final (see, for example, Poulton & Simmonds, 1985). We may suppose that these oscillations are functionally analogous to rats' running from one food-hopper to the other. It is also possible that the process of downloading the probability in humans goes on by eyes movement.

The model of the subject with internality is based on an assumption that a procedure of choice between the positive and negative poles is asymmetrical: if the negative pole is chosen, there is a small probability that the subject will cancel its decision and repeat the process of choice. In MS, the probability of choosing the positive pole is

$$X = \frac{x_1}{x_1 + (1 - x_1)e^{-S}}, \qquad (0.1)$$

where $0 < x_1 < 1$ and $S \geq 0$. Variable x_1 represents the world's pressure toward the positive pole, and S is the *internal variable*. By comparing (0.1) with the equation of the intentional subject (see section 1.4)

$$X = \frac{x_1}{x_1 + (1 - x_1)x_2}, \qquad (0.2)$$

we see that they become similar if we suppose that

$$x_2 = e^{-S}. \qquad (0.3)$$

While deducting (0.1), we made no assumptions concerning human moral choice, therefore, unlike (0.2), the former can be used for the description of not only human behavior, but that of animals as well. Equation (0.1) represents a principle of a live creature's functioning which will be called *the law of internality*:

Behavior is determined both by the environment influence (x_i) and by the internal factor (S) as well.

1. The Law of Internality in a Logical Scheme of Evolution of Behaviorism

In the evolution of the science of behavior, one may see a clear logic which does not depend much on individual preferences of researchers, neither on prohibitions on use the introspective concepts (as for example, Pavlov's avoiding such expression as 'a dog noticed', 'a dog understood', etc.). We single out four stages in the development of behaviorism and can see a move toward the fifth one, today (Fig.1.1). Each stage can be described by a 'law', which expresses the rule of an organism behavior in a concise form.

At the first stage, which originated in the Cartesian time, an organism was represented as a black box with an input and output (we use here a metaphor belonging to later times). An organism's life actions (called responses) correspond to the output, and the environment's demands - to the input. A mechanism inside the box *automatically* transforms each demand into a response. This transformation was called *reflex*.

Pavlov's (1927) discovery that reflexes are of two types: inborn and acquired, indicates the appearance of the second stage. The inborn reflexes were called unconditional, and those acquired as the life experience were called conditional. The majority of probabilistic models belong to the first or second stages. Unlike deterministic models, they describe statistical characteristics of stimulus-response rather than functional relation between a set of stimuli and a set of responses.

During the third stage, it was found that the automatic response to a stimulus may change to become more effective. At the beginning of this stage was Thorndike (1932) who formulated *The Law of Effect*, which shows the ability of a living creature to modify its response to a stimulus depending on its 'effect'. For example, a cat's organism in a Thorndike puzzle box performs selections of successful manipulations with the lock and at the end of successive trials exits cage faster than at the beginning (see also Herrnstein, 1970; Williams, 1988).

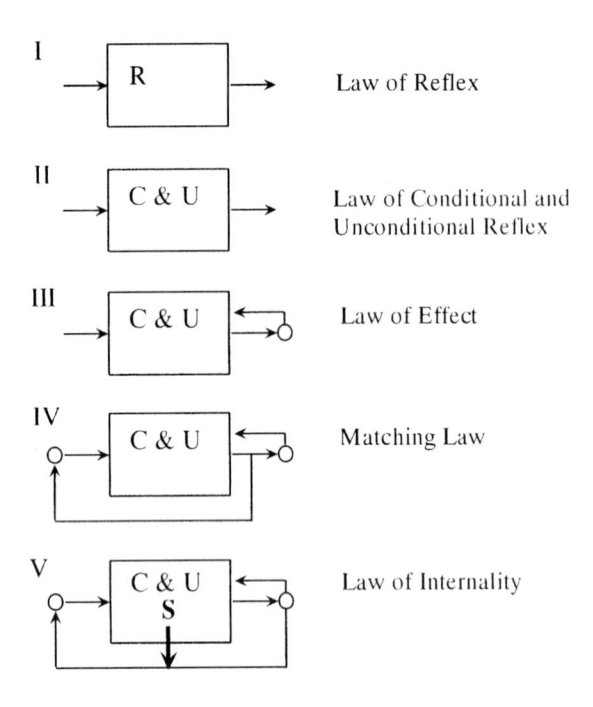

```
I    → [ R ]   →              Law of Reflex

II   → [ C & U ] →            Law of Conditional and
                              Unconditional Reflex

III  → [ C & U ] ⇄            Law of Effect

IV   ○→[ C & U ]⇄             Matching Law
        ↑_____|

V    ○→[ C & U ]⇄             Law of Internality
          S
          ↓
        ↑_____|
```

Fig. 1.1. The logical stages in the development of behaviorism.

The scheme does not reflect the time order of the ideas' appearance. For example, Pavlov, Thorndike, Watson, Bechterev, and Tolman worked on their studies at about the same time, but contributions by early Watson and Bechterev belong to the first stage, by Pavlov to the second one, by Thorndike to the third stage, and by Tolman to the fifth.

The fourth stage is connected with experimental methods developed by Skinner (1938) and his followers. In their experiments, an animal response may influence the generation of stimuli. It turned out that under this condition, an animal generates a line of behavior which establishes a special correlation between a sequence of stimuli and a sequence of responses. A mathematical formula for this correlation has been called the *Matching Law*. Numerous attempts to explain this law in the framework of behaviorism have not given us a convincing explanation.

From the MS point of view, the Matching Law is manifestation of bipolarity and the Law of Internality (Lefebvre, 2002; 2004). But the concept of 'internal variable' lies beyond the vocabulary of behaviorism, and without broadening its vocabulary the science of behavior may not be able to explain the Matching Law. The broadening of behaviorism framework leads us toward the fifth stage, which indicates the acceptance of an idea that a living organism is able to generate acts of behavior whose source lies inside of it (Fig.1.1). This idea is consonant to those of Tolman (1932), but no *theoretical models* have been created based on this idea.

2. The Matching Law

The ability of an organism to regulate relations between the sequence of responses and the sequence of reinforcements was found by Herrnstein (1961) in the experiments with pigeons. A cage had two keys. When a pigeon pecks a key, it may result in the appearance of a grain. Each key has an independent schedule by which reinforcement is delivered. The mean interval between the appearance of grains can vary (Variable-Interval Schedules, *VI*). The experiment consisted of a series of sessions with fixed mean intervals for each key in each session. The pair of intervals was chosen in such a way that sometimes the reinforcement appeared more often in one key, and sometimes in the other.

It turned out that the birds choose the line of behavior such that the ratio of the numbers of pecks to the keys (B_1 and B_2) is approximately equal to the ratio of the numbers of corresponding reinforcements (r_1 and r_2):

$$\frac{B_2}{B_1} = \frac{r_2}{r_1}. \tag{2.1}$$

Equation (2.1) was called the *Matching Law*. There were also experiments with rats and humans. Besides *VI* other schedules were also used. For example, in Variable-Ratio Schedule, *VR*, the mean number of pecks, necessary to receive reinforcement, varied. The results of the experiments led to the formulation of the Generalized Matching Law (Baum, 1974):

$$\frac{B_2}{B_1} = c\left(\frac{r_2}{r_1}\right)^{\beta}, \tag{2.2}$$

where c and β are parameters, which characterize a subject in a given experiment consisting of a sequence of sessions. This equation is usually written in a logarithmic form:

$$\log\frac{B_2}{B_1} = \beta \log\frac{r_2}{r_1} + \log c. \tag{2.3}$$

Quite recently, Baum (Baum et al., 1999; Baum, 2002) put forth a hypothesis, based on the experiment, about the existence of two patterns of behavior, and equation (2.3) being their approximation (see Fig.2.1).

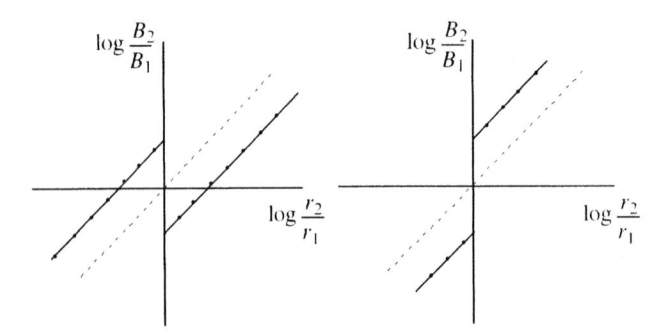

Fig. 2.1. Baum's patterns.

The left graph corresponds to $\beta < 1$, and the right one to $\beta > 1$, if we approximate the data with equation (2.3).

Further, by using MS we will deduce the exact theoretical equation for the Matching Law. We will also demonstrate how to deduce the three patterns of behavior, two of which coincide with those in Fig.2.1, from that theoretical equation.

3. The Attempts to Explain the Matching Law within the Framework of the Science of Behavior

Why does equation (2.3) hold, at least approximately? It is natural to assume that it is a by-product of more fundamental processes (Williams, 1988). Baum and Aparicio (1999) formulated the dominant point of view as follows: "Despite claims to the contrary, all leading theories about operant choice may be seen as models of optimality" (p.75). The idea of optimality is consonant with the main thesis of behaviorism, in accordance with which an animal is adapting to the environment in a way that it looks rational and goal-oriented.

There are numerous general and experimental arguments *pro* and *contra* the principle of optimality as an explanation for the Matching Law (Williams, 1988; Baum et al., 1999). The results of the experiments, conducted by Mazur (1981), present a serious argument against the principle of optimality. The conditions of the experiments permitted the researchers to easily discover the pigeons' tendency to maximize the amount of food they received. Nevertheless, the birds did not choose the optimal strategy; they chose the strategies to make equation (2.3) hold instead.

Let us consider one more argument against the principle of optimality. Equations (2.2) and (2.3), which describe the Generalized Matching Law, have two *free* parameters c and β. Their value must be found experimentally for each subject. There were many discussions concerning β (Baum, 1979; Wearden & Burgess, 1982; Aparicio, 2001), but c was considered just a scale coefficient connecting utility-values of reinforcements from two different sources. A usual explanation of the necessity of its introduction can be clarified with the following example. Let a piece of food from the left food-hopper is 0.75 of that from the right one. If we write (2.1) for the 'sum' of utilities, instead of the number of pieces (r_1 and r_2), we will obtain the following ratio:

$$\frac{B_2}{B_1} = \frac{0.75 r_2}{r_1}. \qquad (3.1)$$

Similar argumentation was used for the experiments in which the pieces of food were equal. In these cases, it was said that parameter c reflects a hidden factor which changes utility-measures of the same product from different sources. Sometimes for the sake of saving this argumentation, the researchers had to assume that the organism of the subject was capable of finding statistical characteristics of non-simultaneous factors and reflecting them onto c. How else could they explain the fixed value of c in the experiments, in which one alternative was connected with schedule *VI*, and the other with schedule *VR*? (See, for example, Baum, 1974, Fig.5.) The explanation of c constant value turns into an independent problem similar, in its complexity, with the explanation of the Matching Law. But if we reject the interpretation of c as a scale coefficient, all the attempts to reduce the Matching Law to optimality look unconvincing.

4. A Model of the Subject with Internality (MS)

The central idea in the science of behavior, if we try to represent it with the help of mathematics, can be reduced to the representation of an organism with a simple function:

$$B = \varphi(z), \qquad (4.1)$$

where B corresponds to the organism's behavior, and z is the external influence. In the early 1930s, it has been already realized that this idea reflects only a very simplified view on an organism (Tolman, 1932). The ways of processing information by an organism are very complex, and the inner environment can be considered as a special factor, to certain degree, independent of the external world. Let S be a variable corresponding to this internal factor, then the organism's behavior is given by the following function of two variables:

$$B = \Psi(z,S).$$

Considering S to be the main variable and z a parameter, we can represent this function as

$$B = \Psi(z,S) = \Phi_z(S). \tag{4.2}$$

Function (4.2) can be specified for the bipolar choice in which one alternative plays the role of the positive pole and the other that of the negative pole. Let us connect variable B with the probability of choosing the positive pole (X), and parameter z with the probability of the environmental 'push' toward the positive pole (x_1). We will write (4.2) as

$$X(S) = \Phi_{x_1}(S), \tag{4.3}$$

where $X(S)$ is a differentiable function, $0 < X < 1$, $0 < x_1 < 1$, and $S \geq 0$. Let

$$X(0) = x_1. \tag{4.4}$$

This condition means that if $S = 0$, the probability of choosing the positive alternative is equal to the probability of the environment's push toward it. Let us designate as X_S the probability with which the system chooses the positive pole, while values of x_1 and S are fixed.

The following axiom makes the distinction between the positive and negative alternatives operational:

The Axiom of Repeated Choice

If at the moment of choice, the internal variable grows from S to $S + \Delta S$ ($0 < \Delta S < 1$; ΔS is considered small) and x_1 does not change, the procedure of choice is as follows. First, the system makes a *preliminary* choice with the probability of choosing the positive pole equal to X_S. If the positive alternative is chosen, the system realizes its choice. If the negative alternative is chosen, then, with a small probability equal to ΔS, the system *cancels* its choice and *repeats* the procedure of choice (with the probability of choosing the positive alternative equal to X_S). The result of the repeated choice is realized no matter which alternative is chosen. (Lefebvre, 2004).

It follows from the Axiom of Repeated Choice that for the values of the internal variable equal to S and $S+\Delta S$, the following trees correspond to the choices (Fig.4.1).

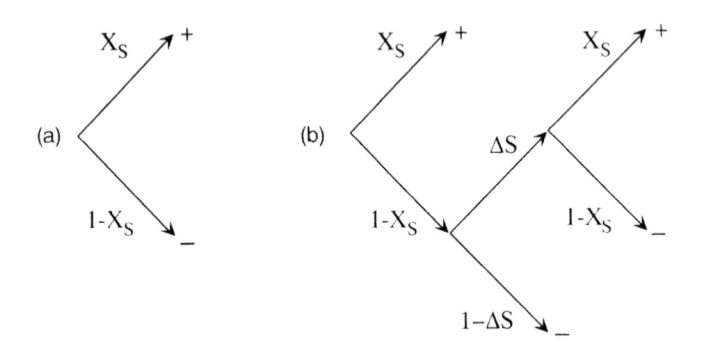

Fig. 4.1. The trees of the choice of the alternative.

(a) For the value of the internal variable equal to S. (b) For the value of the internal variable equal to $S + \Delta S$.

It follows from the tree (b) that

$$X_{S+\Delta S} = X_S + (1 - X_S)\Delta S\, X_S. \tag{4.5}$$

Now we will search for such a differentiable function $X(S)$ (where $X(0) = x_1$) that can be represented as

$$X(S + \Delta S) = X(S) + (1 - X(S))X(S)\Delta S + o(\Delta S), \tag{4.6}$$

where $\dfrac{o(\Delta S)}{\Delta S} \to 0$, if $\Delta S \to 0$. Expression (4.6) can be rewritten as

$$\frac{\Delta X(S)}{\Delta S} = (1 - X(S))X(S) + \frac{o(\Delta S)}{\Delta S}.$$

For the limit at $\Delta S \to 0$, we obtain the following differential equation:

$$\frac{dX(S)}{dS} = (1 - X(S))X(S). \tag{4.7}$$

By solving (4.7) under condition $X(0) = x_1$, we find that

$$X = \Phi_{x_1}(S) = \frac{x_1}{x_1 + (1 - x_1)e^{-S}}. \tag{4.8}$$

The organism's choice is described by (4.8), which corresponds to (4.2) for bipolar choice.

There is an inverse function for (4.8):

$$S = \Phi_{x_1}^{-1}(X),$$

which can be found by transforming (4.8):

$$S = \Phi_{x_1}^{-1}(X) = \ln\frac{1 - x_1}{x_1} - \ln\frac{1 - X}{X}, \tag{4.9}$$

where $\ln\alpha = \log_e\alpha$.

Equation (4.9) allows us to establish a deep relation between the system's internal variable, S, and Shannon's entropy of the system's input and output. Shannon's entropy of the input is

$$H(x_1) = -x_1 \ln x_1 - (1 - x_1)\ln(1 - x_1), \tag{4.10}$$

and that of the output is

$$H(X) = -X \ln X - (1 - X) \ln(1 - X). \tag{4.11}$$

After direct differentiation we obtain

$$\frac{\partial H(x_1)}{\partial x_1} = \ln\frac{1 - x_1}{x_1}, \quad \frac{\partial H(X)}{\partial X} = \ln\frac{1 - X}{X}, \tag{4.12}$$

and by substituting the derivatives' expressions from (4.12) to (4.9), we finally have

$$S = \frac{\partial H(x_1)}{\partial x_1} - \frac{\partial H(X)}{\partial X}. \qquad (4.13)$$

We will introduce now an assumption that will be called *Entropic*: with *fixed* value of S, the system regulates a difference between the entropy derivatives of input and of output such that equation (4.13) holds. In this way, an organism closes itself in the state, in which his choice is described by function (4.8), following from the Axiom of Repeated Choice. The Entropic assumption allows extension of the model to a case with $n \geq 2$ alternatives[1].

For the sake of convenience we rewrite equation (4.9) as follows

$$\ln \frac{1-X}{X} = \ln \frac{1-x_1}{x_1} - S. \qquad (4.14)$$

5. A Deduction of a Theoretical Equation for the Matching Law

Let the alternatives be polarized for an animal in an experimental chamber. Thus, a push to one pedal is the addressing to the positive pole, and a push to another pedal is the addressing to the negative pole. N_1 designates the number of the appeals to the positive alternative within *one* session, and N_2 the number of addressing to the negative alternative within the same session. Numbers n_1 and n_2 are the numbers of reinforcements received from the positive and negative alternatives within *one* session. Let us introduce variables p and q:

$$p = \frac{N_1}{N_1 + N_2} \quad \text{and} \quad q = \frac{n_1}{n_1 + n_2}$$

and let

$$X = p, \; x_1 = q. \qquad (5.1)$$

---

[1] A detailed explanation is given in the Note

Now equation (4.14) can be rewritten as the following 'law':

$$\ln\frac{N_2}{N_1} = \ln\frac{n_2}{n_1} - S, \qquad (5.2)$$

or

$$\frac{N_2}{N_1} = e^{-S}\frac{n_2}{n_1}, \qquad (5.3)$$

where $S \geq 0$. By comparing (5.2) with an empirically found (2.3), we see their similarity, if we consider that B_1 and r_1 correspond to the positive pole, B_2 and r_2 to the negative one, and $\beta = 1$. Further we will give the arguments that equation (5.2) is the 'true' theoretical expression of the Matching Law.

6. Frequencies as Traces of Probabilities Regulation

In equations (5.1), we equalized things that are different in principle: the probabilities with the frequencies. Variables X and x_1, which characterize a system with internality have the meaning of probabilities and can refer only to an *instant* state of the system. Using the quantum-mechanical metaphor, we can say that they correspond to a *mixed* state of a system in a given moment. On the other hand, variables p and q are the frequencies, they describe not an instant state but the entire history of the subject's behavior in the course of one session. They are the characteristics of a process that is not necessarily stochastic. We will describe now a hypothetical cognitive mechanism which generates the subject's mixed state and transforms frequencies into probabilities (see Fig.6.1).

In one session, a sequence of white and black circles corresponds to the subject's responses to the positive and negative alternatives. A sequence of white and black triangles corresponds to reinforcements, The triangle color depends on the color of the alternative from which the reinforcement is received: white designates the positive alternative, and black designates the negative alternative. The circles without triangles above are the responses without reinforcement. (In the real experiments, reinforcements appear more rare than in Fig.6.1) The two 'boxes' correspond to two sections of the memory. The traces of reinforcement are saved in the left section, and the traces of responses are saved in the right one.

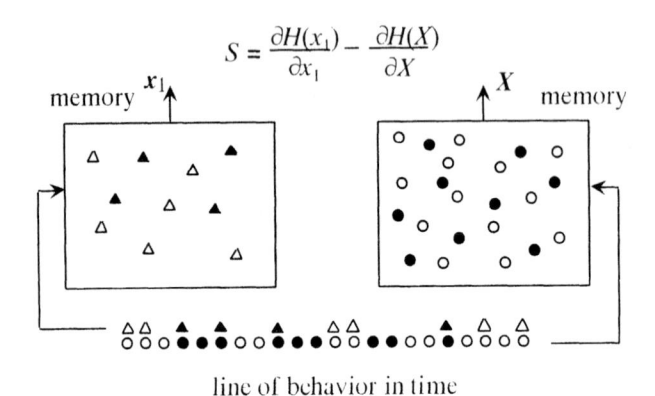

$$S = \frac{\partial H(x_1)}{\partial x_1} - \frac{\partial H(X)}{\partial X}$$

line of behavior in time

Fig. 6.1. A hypothetical scheme of information processing.

The triangles correspond to the reinforcements: the whites from the positive alternative, the blacks from the negative one. The circles correspond to the responses: white to the positive and black to the negative alternatives. For fixed S, the system maintains relation (4.13) in each session, and as a result the value of function (4.8) is being computed.

We assume that system *remembers neither* the *order* of responses and reinforcements *nor* the *correspondence* between them. For example, the system cannot determine which white circle corresponds to a particular white triangle. Therefore, a 'lump' of white and black triangles is located in the left section, and a 'lump' of white and black circles are in the right one.

Let randomized flashes of 'recollection' appear in a cognitive system. Each reminiscence corresponds either to a flash of one circle or of one triangle. Flashes of triangles and circles do not depend on each other. White triangles flash with the probability x_1, and white circles flash with the probability X; probability x_1 is a characteristic of an input, and probability X is that of an output of the system with internality. The goal of the organism is to maintain relation (4.13) unchanged under condition of fixed S. How this can be done? Suppose (4.13) does not hold. This may happen because the number of white circles in the right part of the memory is either too small or too large. If it is too small, the organism addresses to the positive alternative and adds the white circles to the memory until (4.13) is restored. If the number is too large, the organism addresses to the negative alternative and supplements the memory with black circles to restore (4.13). This strategy is always successful because the subject in the experimental chamber receives very scarce reinforcements, that is, the triangles appear very rarely. Therefore, the organism can always compensate distortion in (4.13) by adding to the right box either white or black circles. We see that regulation in this system is such that the *frequencies* of quasi-random sequences of reinforcements and responses automatically turn into *probabilities* of 'memory flashes', since the number of white circles in the memory box and in the behavior line equal to each other. The same is true for black circles and for white and black triangles (see Fig.6.1). This consideration explains the relation between frequencies and probabilities given by (5.1).

In accordance with our hypothesis, by maintaining the relation between reinforcements and responses given by (4.13), the subject keeps his mixed state, that is, the state of uncertainty, in which he is ready to choose the positive pole with the probability

$$X = \frac{x_1}{x_1 + (1 - x_1)e^{-S}}, \qquad (6.1)$$

where S is constant during all the sessions.

How is an uncertain state connected to the procedure of repeated choice? Suppose that in real experiments, there are small fluctuations of the value of the internal variable, S, and it can take on any value from the small interval $[M_1, M_2]$, where $M_1 < M_2$. In the scheme given in Fig.6.1, the value of the internal variable is equal to the minimal value, that is, $S=M_1$. If at the moment of the instantaneous choice, the value of the internal variable is equal to $M_1+\Delta S$, then the system makes its preliminary choice with the probability $X(M_1)$ of choosing the positive alternative, and $1 - X(M_1)$ of choosing the negative one. If the positive alternative is chosen, the system realizes its choice, if the negative alternative is chosen, the system repeats its choice with the small probability equal to ΔS. Function (6.1) has an advantage over other functions, because with small ΔS, the procedure of the repeated choice gives its approximation to within $o(\Delta S)$.

7. Function of the Uncertain State

We assume that the subject has a 'super task' to which he is preparing itself by turning sometimes to the positive and sometimes to the negative alternative. Our hypothesis is as follows:

An organism prepares the self to the possibility of instant choice between the positive and negative alternatives in a critical moment of its life.

In the experimental chamber, an animal choice is limited by two alternatives. For example, the positive pole corresponds to the better protected alternative which is poorer in food supply. In a moment of sudden danger, the animal would choose the positive alternative with the probability X and the negative one with the probability $1 - X$. Thus, continuous run of the animal between the food- hoppers is a cognitive computational process which involves the entire organism. The goal of this process is not only a search for food, but also the formation and maintaining of an uncertain state for a possible instantaneous choice in the future (as was mentioned in the Introduction). In other words, the animal behavior in the experimental chamber that corresponds to law (5.3) is a process of an organism preparation of its probabilistic response.

8. Prediction of Behavioral Patterns

Suppose that interval $[M_1, M_2]$ is fixed for each subject on the entire set of sessions. We will call an alternative *richer with food*, if a subject generates the line of behavior such that this alternative is reinforced more often. Consider now three possible relations between the alternative's 'richness' and its polarity.

A. One alternative plays the role of the positive pole independently from being more or less reinforced in a particular sessions.

B. In each session, the alternative that is *less reinforced* plays the role of the positive pole.

C. In each session, the alternative that is *more reinforced* plays the role of the positive pole.

Independently from polarization, one alternative will be called 'right', and the other 'left'. Let B_1 and B_2 be the numbers of 'appeals' to the right and left alternatives, and r_1 and r_2 be the numbers of reinforcements from the right and left alternatives, respectively. With the help of (5.2), we construct graphs which connect $\ln \frac{B_2}{B_1}$ and $\ln \frac{r_2}{r_1}$ for each case.

(A) Let the right alternative play the role of the positive pole in all sessions. Then $B_1=N_1$, $B_2=N_2$, $r_1=n_1$, $r_2=n_2$, and equation (5.2) can be represented as

$$\ln \frac{B_2}{B_1} = \ln \frac{r_2}{r_1} - S. \qquad (8.1)$$

If the left alternative plays the role of the positive pole in all sessions, $B_1=N_2$, $B_2=N_1$, $r_1=n_2$, $r_2=n_1$, and equation (5.2) is:

$$\ln \frac{B_1}{B_2} = \ln \frac{r_1}{r_2} - S, \qquad (8.2)$$

or

$$\ln \frac{B_2}{B_1} = \ln \frac{r_2}{r_1} + S. \qquad (8.3)$$

The graphs in Fig.8.1 correspond to equations (8.1) and (8.3).

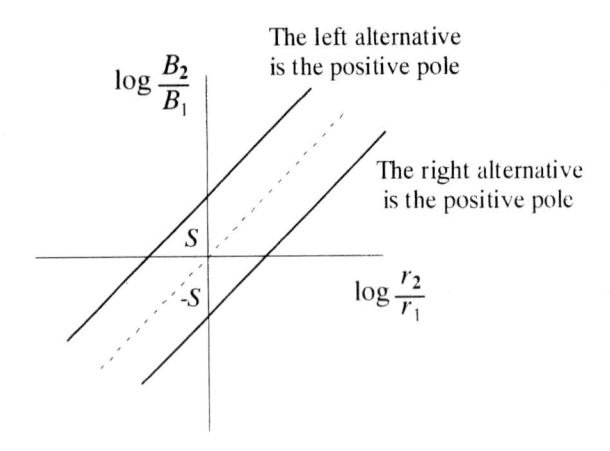

Fig. 8.1. Pattern A.

An alternative plays the role of the positive pole independently from being more or less rich with food in each particular session.

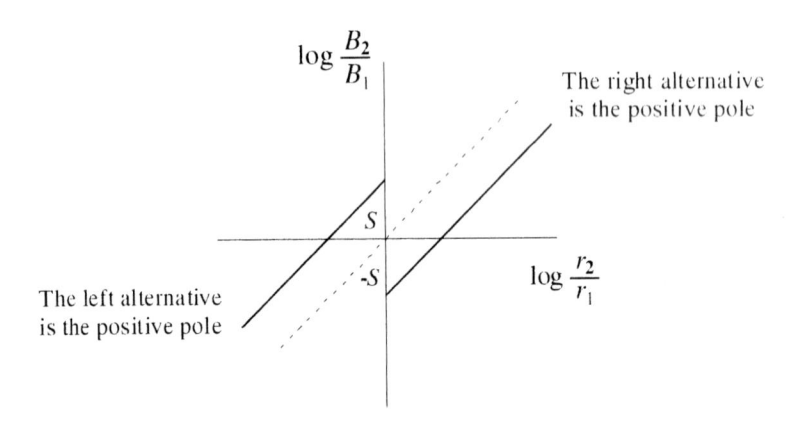

Fig. 8.2. Pattern B.

In each session, the alternative that is less rich with food plays the role of the positive pole.

(B) In this case, the right (or left) alternative plays the role of the positive pole only in those sessions in which it is less reinforced. The right-hand side of the horizontal axis corresponds to $r_2 > r_1$, and the left-hand side to $r_2 < r_1$. When $r_2 > r_1$, the right alternative plays the role of the positive pole, and when $r_2 < r_1$, the left one does. The graph in Fig.8.2 corresponds to this case.

(C) This is the case, in which the right (or left) alternative plays the role of the positive pole in those sessions in which it is better reinforced. When $r_2 > r_1$, the left alternative plays the role of the positive pole, and when $r_2 < r_1$, the right one does it (Fig.8.3)

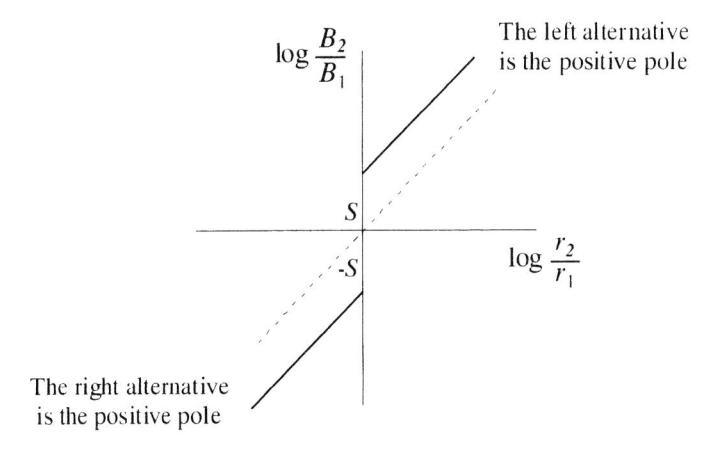

Fig. 8.3. Pattern C.

In each session, the alternative that is richer with food plays the role of the positive pole.

We see that for cases (B) and (C) the graph discontinues at $r_2 = r_1$. These patterns were experimentally found by Baum (2002); they are given in Fig.2.1. Pattern (A) is independent and cannot be reduced to the two others. It appears in those cases, when one alternative significantly differs from the other, for example, the right one is connected with schedule *VR*, and the left one with *VI*. Then the *VR* alternative plays the role of the positive pole, and the *VI* alternative that of the negative pole (this follows from an analysis of the experimental data obtained by

Baum (1974) and Baum & Aparicio (1999)). Pattern B is realized under conditions that the alternatives differ only by the rate of reinforcements. Finally, pattern (C) is observed when under conditions of the experiment, the change of the alternatives is made difficult.

Pattern (B) poses a serious problem: why the alternative which is poorer with food can play the role of the positive pole and the one richer with food that of the negative? We will consider this problem further.

9. Animals' Deontological Evaluations

We would like to put forth a hypothesis that animals have ability to make bipolar, positive *vs.* negative evaluations analogous to (and perhaps evolutionary preceding of) the human moral evaluation good *vs.* bad. To find out how moral-like evaluations in animals are connected with the utilitarian preferences, let us consider ourselves first.

Here is a specific case. In 1918, during the Civil War in Russia, the head of one family ends up in China, while his wife is left in Russia with six children; she is executed. The father meets a wealthy American, who with the risk to his life goes to Russia, finds children and brings all six of them to their father to China. Ten years later, with great difficulties, the same American helps them to move to the USA. The oldest of the saved children feels disappointed there.

> Why America was not good for twenty-two-year-old Mulia? Nostalgia? No. The thing was that the most important value for her - that of *self-sacrifice* - contradicted to the American style of life. Mulia was confused. An idea of 'living for others', natural to her, somehow could not be applied to America. Of course, Mr. Crane 'sacrificed' a lot of time and money to charity (he was helping 50 more families to stand on their feet!). But his activity did not carry that special beauty of total self-sacrifice, admiration of which Mulia got with her mother's milk? (Pann. The Older Daughter. *Novoye Russkoye Slovo*, May 24-25, 2003.)

Let us suppress our surprise (and perhaps, indignation) of the lack of psychological grace in this young woman. We will try to analyze this example from a naturalist's point of view. What feature in Mr. Crane behavior was unacceptable for Mulia? This highly noble man helped fifty-one families. It is clear that he had to plan his activity and *count money* spent on each family. In other words, his *good deals were connected with money*, this is why his activity lacked 'that special beauty of self-sacrifice'. It looks as if this young woman has an automatic mechanism inside her which forbids combining utilitarian and deontological evaluations

We make now the next step and suppose that this mechanism has a deep biological nature, while it only looks culturally conditioned. In developing this idea we can hypothesize that birds and mammals have two systems of evaluations. The first system, *utilitarian*, reflects evaluations of the utility-measures of the alternatives connected with the *animal close biological needs*. The second one, *deontological*, is connected with bipolar evaluations positive-negative on a larger time scale.

Consider, for example, a hungry animal choosing between two food-hoppers. The first one contains more food, but the second one is safer (say, hidden from view). In this case, the feeder richer with food gets evaluation 'negative', while the poorer one receives 'positive' evaluation. Thus, animals' 'idealism' while being related to specific life-important evaluations, is nevertheless separated from this-minute preferences. We cannot exclude the possibility that this distinction is supported by a special mental mechanism, whose work in humans reveals itself in a dramatic contrast between material and ideal values. In bipolar choice, this mechanism 'ennobles' the alternative which is less connected with the utility of this very minute.

From this point of view, let us look at the patterns of behavior described in the previous sections. Pattern (B) appears when the left and right food-hoppers differ only in their frequency of food delivering. In this case, as we found, the alternative, which is *less* reinforced, plays the role of the positive pole. We may hypothesize that this phenomenon reflects the work of the same mechanism which counterposes 'dirty' money and 'pure' intentions in humans. The alternative polarization opposite to their utilitarian preferences as food sources is analogous to the human act of *purification*, that is, of separation good from practical profit. Let us emphasize that this happens if the alternatives differ only in the frequency of food delivery. If some 'non-utilitarian' factor exists, which predetermines polarization of the alternatives, then the polarization remains the same for the entire set of sessions independently from reinforcement of the positive alternative. This conclusion results from the interpretation of pattern (A).

10. Sacred Shift

Altruism is understood as spending one's own resources in order to help others. But this is not the only form of sacrificial behavior. Voluntary expenditure of one's finances and energy related to creation and support of religious and moral symbols is another form of sacrificial behavior. Everyone can cite an example of people who agree to perform work connected with higher values (say, building a cathedral) for free or for smaller pay than they would require for similar work not connected with these values. Now we can explain this phenomenon. During the process of the subject's forming and maintaining a mixed state, the alternatives play the role of special agencies where the subject can apply for food. If we interpret N_1 and N_2 in (5.3) as the subject's *expenditures* of appeals to the positive and negative agencies, and n_1 and n_2 as his revenues, then the ratios

$$\frac{n_1}{N_1} \text{ and } \frac{n_2}{N_2} \qquad (10.1)$$

express the mean payments the subject requires from the agencies for one appeal. It follows from (5.3) that

$$\frac{n_1}{N_1} \leq \frac{n_2}{N_2}. \qquad (10.2)$$

Therefore, it turns out that on average, the subject never requires more goods for one appeal from the positive agency than from the negative one. This conclusion is true not only for humans but for the rats and pigeons, as well.

Conclusion

We are convinced that we have a mental domain. This belief is based only on our own subjective experience. We do not have an *operational criterion* which would allow us to find out whether a particular organism or a technical device has an inner world, or are we observing an 'inanimate' physical process. This problem extends beyond the framework of science and touches upon the core of our morality. We believe that a rat and a pigeon are able to suffer. But what about a fish or a bee, can they suffer? The results described in this Part suggest a hypothesis that in evolution, the mental domain in living creatures appears at the same time as their ability to make a probabilistic choice. We also substantiated an assumption that the creatures with mental domain can 'self-program'. In other words, they can program themselves by downloading the values of probabilities with which they will make their choice. Furthermore, we have shown that the Matching Law is an external demonstration of this self-programming. If this hypothesis proves to be correct, then the Matching Law will turn into an operational criterion. We will thus have grounds to consider organisms, for which it holds, to have a mental domain.

A Note to the Additional Part

Equation (4.13), which connects the system internal variable with the input entropy and the output entropy, can be expanded into an arbitrary number of the alternative (Lefebvre, 2004). A simplest case is, when one alternative is related to the positive pole and all others to the negative pole. In this case, X is interpreted as the probability of choosing the positive alternative, and $1-X$ as the probability of choosing a negative alternative. Let us note that in this case the model does not allow us to predict the distribution of probabilities of choosing each negative alternative.

The model also can be expanded to the case when one alternative is related to the negative pole and all others to the positive pole. We will consider this case in more detail.

Let k be the number of all alternatives arbitrary numbered but the negative alternative has number k. The following system is a generalization of equation (4.13):

$$S_j = \frac{\partial}{\partial q_j} H(q_1,...,q_{k-1}) - \frac{\partial}{\partial p_j} H(p_1,...,p_{k-1}) \; ; \tag{1}$$

$S_j \geq 0;\ 1 > q_i > 0;\ 1 > p_i > 0;\ i = 1, 2, ..., k;\ j = 1, 2, ..., k\text{-}1;\ k \geq 2;$

$$\sum_{i=1}^{k} q_i = 1, \quad \sum_{i=1}^{k} p_i = 1 \; ; \tag{i}$$

$$H(q_1,...,q_{k-1}) = -\sum_{i=1}^{k} q_i \ln q_i \; ; \tag{ii}$$

$$H(p_1,...,p_{k-1}) = -\sum_{i=1}^{k} p_i \ln p_i \; , \tag{iii}$$

where $q_1, ..., q_k$ is distribution of probabilities of the environment jolts toward the alternatives, and $p_1, ..., p_k$ is distribution of probabilities of the subject's choosing the alternatives. Distribution $q_1, q_2, ..., q_k$ describes the system input, and $p_1, p_2, ..., p_k$ the system output. The work of the subject's cognitive system consists of establishing and maintaining equations (1) under condition that internal variables $S_1, ..., S_{k-1}$ have constant values.

In order to acquire an operational meaning, the system (1) needs us to establish the connections between variables' changes under condition that normalization (i) holds. We assume that when the value of q_m, ($m < k$), which refers to one of the positive alternatives, is changing to ε, ($\varepsilon = o(q_k)$), none of q_j, ($j < k, j \neq m$), which refer to other positive alternatives, changes. There are some other changes, however: the value of q_k that refers to the negative alternative changes to $-\varepsilon$. We make similar assumption about p_j. It is clear that with these connections between variables, normalization (i) holds. We say that the positive alternatives are *locally independent*, if the probabilities distribution change only as described above.

For the system, in which positive alternatives are locally independent, the following equations hold:

$$\frac{\partial}{\partial q_j} H(q_1, ... q_{k-1}) = \ln \frac{q_k}{q_j} \quad , j = 1, 2, ..., k-1, \qquad (2)$$

$$\frac{\partial}{\partial p_j} H(p_1, ... p_{k-1}) = \ln \frac{p_k}{p_j} \quad , j = 1, 2, ..., k-1. \qquad (3)$$

Thus, (1) can be rewritten as follows:

$$S_j = \ln \frac{q_k}{q_j} - \ln \frac{p_k}{p_j} \quad , j = 1, 2, ..., k-1. \qquad (4)$$

By solving (4), we obtain

$$p_j = \frac{q_j e^{S_j}}{\sum_{i=1}^{k-1} q_i e^{S_i} + q_k}, \; j = 1, 2, ..., k\text{-}1. \qquad (5)$$

A set of function (5) is compatible with the assumption concerning a local independency of the positive alternatives (see Lefebvre, 2004).

Let us introduce now $(k\text{-}1)$-dimensional Euclidian space and consider Shannon's functions $H(q_1,...,q_{k-1})$ and $H(p_1,...,p_{k-1})$ as potential functions. System of equations (1) can be rewritten in vector form as follows:

$$grad \; H(p_1, ..., p_{k-1}) = grad \; H(q_1, ..., q_{k-1}) - S, \qquad (6)$$

where

$$grad \; H(p_1,...,p_{k-1}) = \left(\ln \frac{p_k}{p_1}, ..., \ln \frac{p_k}{p_{k-1}} \right) = A, \qquad (7)$$

$$grad \; H(q_1,...,q_{k-1}) = \left(\ln \frac{q_k}{q_1}, ..., \ln \frac{q_k}{q_{k-1}} \right) = B, \qquad (8)$$

$$S = (S_1, S_2, ..., S_{k-1}). \qquad (9)$$

Vectors B and S may be regarded at as 'forces' applied to the subject. The source of force B is the external world, and the source of force S is located inside the subject. The resulting vector A represents the force applied by subject to the external world. These forces constitute fields that will be called *entro-fields*. Condition

$$q_1 = q_1 = ... = q_k = 1/k$$

corresponds to the situation, when the frequencies of jolts toward each alternative are equal. In this case, as it follows from (8), vector B is a zero-vector:

$$B = grad \; H(q_1, ..., q_{k-1}) = (0, ..., 0), \qquad (10)$$

and the vector of the subject's activity is

$$grad\ H(p_1, ..., p_{k-1}) = -(S_1, ..., S_{k-1}), \qquad (11)$$

i.e., it depends only on the internal variables.

The probabilities of jolts toward alternatives

$$q_1, q_2, ..., q_k;\ q_i > 0, \qquad (12)$$

can be regarded at as the alternatives' normalized *utility-measures*. They show situation-limited significance of the alternatives for the subject that are not connected with their polarization.

And the following values:

$$e^{S_1}, e^{S_2}, ..., e^{S_{k-1}}, 1;\ S_i \geq 0, \qquad (13)$$

are called the alternatives' *purities*. They reflect non-situational significance of the alternatives for the subject (the purity of the negative alternative is equal to 1). For example, the alternative may be differently connected with religious, moral or some other general factors significant to the subject and predetermining the values of the internal variables $S_1, ..., S_{k-1}$.

Looking at equation (5), we see that the probability of alternatives' choice is proportional to the following values

$$q_1 e^{S_1}, q_2 e^{S_2}, ..., q_{k-1} e^{S_{k-1}}, q_k, \qquad (14)$$

each of which is a product of corresponding utility-measure and purity. The values in (14) will be called preference-measures or *preferences*. They reflect a combined effect of situational and deontological importance of each alternative for the subject. It is easy to see that if the value of any single S_m grows infinitely, the probability of choosing this particular alternative tends to 1, even if its situational utility-measure is negligible. Equation (5) describes relation between utilitarian and deontological aspects.

Bibliography to the Additional Part

Aparicio, C. F. Overmatching in Rats: The Barrier Choice Paradigm. *Journal of the Experimental Analysis of Behavior*, **75**, 93-106, 2001.

Atkinson, R. C., Bower, G. H., and Crothers, E. J. *An Introduction to Mathematical Learning Theory*. New York: Wiley, 1965.

Audley, R. J. A Stochastic Model for Individual Choice Behavior. *Psychological Review*, **67**, 1-15, 1960

Baum, W. M. On Two Types of Deviation from the Matching Law: Bias and Undermatching. *Journal of the Experimental Analysis of Behavior*, **22**, 231-242., 1974.

_____. Matching, Undermatching, and Overmatching in Studies of Choice. *Journal of the Experimental Analysis of Behavior*, **32**, 269-281, 1979.

_____. From Molecular to Molar: A Paradigm Shift In Behavior Analysis. *Journal of the Experimental Analysis of Behavior*, **78**, 95-116, 2002.

Baum, W. M. & Aparicio, C. F. Optimality and Concurrent Variable-Interval and Variable-Ratio Schedules. *Journal of the Experimental Analysis of Behavior*, **71**, 75-89,1999.

Baum, W. M., Schwendiman, J. W., and Bell, K. E. Choice, Contingency Discrimination, and Foraging Theory. *Journal of the Experimental Analysis of Behavior*, **71**, 355-373, 1999.

Bower, G. H. Choice-Point Behavior. In: Bush, R. R. & Estes, W. K. (Eds.), *Studies in Mathematical Learning Theory*, Stanford: Stanford University Press, 1959.

Bradley, R. A. & Terry, M. E. Rank Analysis of Incomplete Block Design. The Method of Paired Comparisons I. *Biometrika*, **39**, 324-345, 1952.

Davidson, D., Suppes, P., and Siegel, S. *Decision Making*. Stanford: Stanford University Press, 1957.

Herrnstein, R. J. Relative and Absolute strength of Response As a Function of Frequency of Reinforcement. *Journal of the Experimental Analysis of Behavior*, **4**, 267-272, 1961.

_____. On the Law of Effect. *Journal of the Experimental Analysis of Behavior*, **13**, 243-266, 1970.

LaBerge, D. L. A Recruitment Theory of Simple Behavior. *Psychometrika*, **27**, 375-396, 1962.

Lefebvre, V. A. *A Psychological Theory of Bipolarity and Reflexivity*. Lewiston, N.Y.: The Edwin Mellen Press, 1992.

_____. Categorization, Operant Matching, and Moral Choice. Institute for Mathematical and Behavioral Sciences, *MBS*, **99-14**, UCI, 1999.

_____. The Law of Self-Reflexion. *Journal of Reflexive Processes and Control*, **1**, 2, 91-100, 2002.

_____. Bipolarity, Choice, and Entro-Field. In: *PROCEEDINGS. The 8th World Multi-Conference on Systemics, Cybernetics and Informatics* Vol. IV, pp.95-99, 2004.

Luce, R. D. *Individual choice Behavior: A Theoretical Analysis*. New York: Wiley, 1959.

Mazur, J. E. Optimization Theory Fails to Predict Performance of Pigeons in a Two-Response Situation. *Science*, **214**, 823-825, 1981.

Mosteller, F. & Nogee, P. An Experimental Measurement of Utility. *The Journal of Political Economy*, **59**, 371-404, 1951.

Pavlov, I. P. *Conditioned Reflexes*. Oxford: Oxford University Press, 1927.

Poulton, E. S. & Simmonds, D. C. V. Subjective Zeros, Subjectively Equal Stimulus Spacing, and Contraction Biases in Very First Judgments of Lightness. *Perception & Psychophysics*, **37**, 420-428, 1985.

Restle, F. *Psychology of Judgment and Choice*. New York: Wiley, 1961.

Ruddle, H., Bradshaw, C. M., Szabadi, E., and Bevan, P. Behaviour of Humans in Concurrent Schedules Programmed on Spatially Separated Operanda. *Quarterly Journal of Experimental Psychology*, **31**, 509-517, 1979.

Savage, L. J. The Theory of Statistical Decision. *American Statistical Association Journal*, **46**, 55-67, 1951.

Skinner, B. F. *The Behavior of Organisms: An Experimental Analysis.* Appleton-Century-Crofts, 1938.

Spence, K. W. Conceptual Models of Spatial and Non-Spatial Selective Learning. In: Spence, K.W. (Ed.), Behavior Theory and Learning, Englewood Cliffs, N. J.: Prentice-Hall, 1960.

Thorndike, E. L. *Animal Intelligence: An Experimental Study of the Associative Processes in Animals. Psychological Review Monographs Supplement*, Vol.2, No.8, 1911.

Thurstone, L. L. A Law of Comparative Judgment. *Psychology Review*. **34**, 273-286, 1927.

Tolman, E. C. *Purposive Behavior in Animals and Men.* New York: Appleton-Century-Crofts, 1932.

von Neuman, J. & Morgenstern, O. *Theory of Games and Economic Behavior*. Princeton: Princeton University Press, 1947.

Wearden, J. H. & Burgess, I. S. Matching Since Baum (1979). *Journal of the Experimental Analysis of Behavior*, **28**, 339-348, 1982.

Williams, B. A. Reinforcement, Choice, and Response Strength. In: Atkinson, R. C., Herrnstein, R. J., Lindzey, G., Luce, R. D. (Eds.) *Steven's Handbook of Experimental Psychology*, Vol.2, 167-244, 1988.

INDEX OF NAMES

Adams-Webber, J. i, 47, 48, 50, 52, 93, 94, 98, 100
Anderson, N. H. 23, 93
Aparicio, C. F. 113, 126, 135
Archibald, R. C. 53, 93
Atkinson, R. C. 106, 135, 137
Audley, R. J. 106, 135
Ballesteros, S. 98
Balzano, G. J. 63, 93
Banathy, B. 99
Banshchikov, V. M. 100
Barnett, J. D. 40, 93
Baum, W. i, iii, 112-114, 125, 126, 135, 137
Becker, L. A. 28, 94
Bechterev, B. M. 110
Bell, K. E. 135
Benjafield, J. 47, 53, 54, 93, 94
Berlyne, D. E. 53, 94
Bernoulli, D. 60
Berscheid, E. 28, 94
Bevan, P. 136
Bigava, Z. I. 55, 94
Birnbaum, M. H. 23, 94
Bless, E. 28, 95
Bobko, D. J. 54, 100
Bonnano, G. A. 44, 94
Borovik, A. i
Bower, G. H. 106, 135
Bradley, R. A. 106, 135
Bradshaw, C. M. 136
Brock, T. C. 28, 94
Brody, N. 101
Burgess, I. S. 108, 113, 137
Burns, E. M. 58, 94
Bush, R. R. 135

Butler, D. 40, 94
Carlsmith, J.M. 28, 94
Carlson, M. 28, 94
Chavchanidze, V. V. 16, 95
Coan, C. A. 53, 95
Cohen, H. F. 57, 95
Colman, S. 53, 95
Crothers, E. J. 135
D'Alambert 60
da Vinci, L. 53
Daltman, P. E. 53, 101
Darlington, R. B. 28, 95
Davidson, D. 106, 135
Davis, F. C. 53, 54, 95
Davis, S. T. 54, 95
Deutsch, D. 94, 101
Doczi, G. 53, 95
Dowling, W. J. 63, 95
Eilers, R. E. 98
Elfner, L. 61, 95
Epting, F.R. 47, 93, 100
Estes, W. K. 135
Eu, M. F. 40, 95
Euler, L. 60
Fechner, G. T. 53, 95, 96
Feynman, R. P. 61, 95
Fourier, J. 60
Freedman, J. L. 28, 95
Galanter, E. H. 21-24, 89, 101
Galilei, V. 60
Galilei, G. 60
Garamoni, G. L. 47, 100
Garbuzov, N. A. 62, 63, 77, 78, 95
Garfias, R. i, 72, 98
Ghyka, M. C. 53, 95
Glover, J. 6, 95

Godkewitsch, M. 53, 96
Green, T. R. G. 47, 94
Grice, J. 52, 96
Gross, A. 28, 94
Hambidge, J. 53, 93, 96
Harrison, A. A. 43, 96
Harwood, D. L. 63, 95
Helmholtz, H. L. F. 60, 96, 99
Helson, H. 21, 96
Herrnstein, R. J. iii, 105, 110, 111, 136, 137
Hipparchus 27
Jahnke, J. C. 54, 95
Jastrow, J. 27, 96
Jusczyk, P.W. 63, 96
Kahneman, D. 38, 102
Kauff, D. M. 101
Kelly, G. A. 1, 47, 96
Kendall P. C. 100
Kenny, A. 6, 96
Kepler, J. 57
Kessler, E. J. 69, 96
Krueger, L. E. 60, 96
Krueger, F. 23, 96
Krumhansl, C. L. 61, 63, 69, 71, 96, 97
Kunst, J. 72, 97
Kunst-Wilson, W. R. 44, 97
LaBerge, D. L. 106, 136
Lalo, C. 53, 97
Landfield A.W. 93
Le Corbusier 53, 97
Lefebvre, V. A. 14, 48, 60, 65, 72-74, 84, 85, 97-99, 107, 111, 116, 131, 133, 136
Lefebvre, V. D. i, 40, 48, 98
Leichton, R. B. 95
Lerner, M. J. 28, 98, 101
Levelt, W. J. M. 60, 99
Levitin, L. i
Lindzey, G. 137
Lipps, Th. 61, 98
Lockhead, G. R. 54, 55, 98

Losskii, N. 6, 98
Luce, R. D. i, 106, 136, 137
Lynch, M. P. 63, 98
Macker, C. E. 28, 95
Mancuso, J.C. 93
Mandler, G. 44, 98
Marczewska, H. 47, 98
Marks, L. E. 23, 99
Martin, D. W. 61, 102
Matthews, G. 28, 98
Mazur, J. E. 113, 136
McClain, E. i, 57, 60, 97, 99
McDaniel, B. L. 96
McGoveran, D. 16, 99
McGraw, K. M. 41, 99
Messick, D. M.47, 99
Meyer, M. F. 61, 99
Michelson, L. 47, 101
Miller, N. 28, 94
Morgenstern, O. 106, 137
Mosteller, F. 106, 136
Mozart, W. A. 63
Nadirashvili, S. A. 94
Nakamura, Y. 98
Newton, I. 60
Nogee, P. 106, 136
O'Kelly, J. i
Oller, D. R. 98
Orlov, Yu. F. 16, 99
Osgood, C. E. 1, 48, 99
Oshins, E. 16, 99
Parducci, A. 21, 24, 25, 99
Pavlov, I. P. 109, 110, 136
Piehl, J. 53, 99
Plato 57, 60, 97, 99
Plomp, R. 60, 99
Plug, C. 53, 54, 100
Pomeroy, E. 54, 94
Popper, K. i, 103
Poulton, E. C. 41-43, 90, 100, 108, 136
Pythagoras 61, 62
Ranney, A. 40, 94, 100

Rapoport, A. i
Regan, J. W. 28, 100
Restle, F. 106, 136
Reznik, V. I. 100
Rigdon, M. A. 47, 100
Rodney, Y. 48, 93
Romany, S. 47, 100
Rotar, V. i
Ruddle, H. 108, 136
Sadalla, E. 28, 102
Sands, M. 95
Saunders, M.A. 54, 94
Savage, L. J. 106, 137
Schiffman, H. R. 54, 100
Schmidt, S. i
Schreider, Yu. i
Schwartz, R. M. 47, 100, 101
Schwendiman, J. W. 135
Seamon, J. G. 44, 101
Shepard, R. N. 61, 97, 101
Shepp, B.E. 98
Shipley, W. C. 53, 101
Siegel, S. 106, 135
Simmonds, D. C. V. 41-43, 90, 100, 108, 136
Simmons, C. H. 28, 101
Skinner, B. F. 111, 137
Spence, K. W. 106, 137
Steele, B. A. 53, 101
Stevens, S. S. 21, 22-24, 26-28, 89, 96, 101
Stevin, S. 57
Stillings, N. A. 94
Stradling, S. G. 48, 102

Stumpf, C. 61, 101
Suci, G. J. 48, 99
Suppes, P. 106, 135
Svensson, L. T. 54, 101
Szabadi, E. 136
Tannenbaum, P. H. 48, 99
Terhardt, E. 61, 101
Terry, M. F. 106, 135
Thompsen, D. 96
Thompson, G. G. 53, 101
Thorndike, E. L. 110, 137
Thurstone, L. L. 106, 137
Tolman, E. C. 110, 111, 114, 137
Trehub, S. E. 63, 102
Tuohy, A. P. 48, 102
Tversky, A. 38, 102
Tyntarev, K. i
Urbano, R. C. 98
Valentine, C. W. 53, 102
VanZandt, B. J. S. 98
von Neuman, J. 106, 137
Wallace, J. 28, 102
Wallington, S. S. 27, 95
Walster, E. 27, 94
Ward, W. D. 58, 61, 95, 96, 102
Warren, R. M. 41, 100
Watson, J. B. 110
Wearden, J. H. 108, 113, 137
Wegener, B. 94
Wheeler, H. 98
Williams, B. A. 105, 110, 113, 137
Zajonc, R. B. 43, 44, 91, 97, 102
Zarlino, G. 57
Zhukovin, V. E. 95

SUBJECT INDEX

altruism 28, 101, 128
axiom of
    credulity 5-7
    free will 5-7
    non-evil intent 5-7
    repeated choice 115, 116, 118
behaviorism 105, 109, 110, 111, 113
belief 13, 15, 16, 34, 37, 38, 41, 48,
    50, 51, 61, 129
    index of 15, 32, 37, 41, 43, 44,
        45, 50, 51, 73
    intensity of 3
    pole of 37, 38, 41, 43-45, 50,
        51
bipolar choice 3, 105, 115, 117, 127
bipolarity 1, 111, 136
categorization 1, 21, 22, 23, 25, 26,
    40, 47, 63, 136
    cross-cultural 64
construct 3, 38, 40, 41, 42, 47-51, 54,
    93, 96. 100, 107
diatonic 63
    scales 63
    context 63, 97
entro-fields 133, 136
entropy 3, 117, 118, 131
ethical status 84
evaluations 15, 27, 40-42, 44, 45, 47,
    49, 50, 89-91, 126, 127
    deontological 126, 127
    of others 47, 49, 50-52
feeling 14, 32, 75
    inner 3, 14, 100
    of intention 14
    of the self 14
    of the world 14, 33
fixed point 4, 10, 21, 31

free will 1, 3, 4-6, 96, 98
gamma-algebra 2, 85-88
golden section 35, 38, 40-43, 45, 47,
    48, 52-55, 79, 93-102
graphic metaphor 13
image of
    the other 81, 87, 88
    the group 81, 82
    the self 1, 3, 8-10, 13-15, 32,
        81, 83, 84, 87
    the world 3, 4, 14, 15, 21, 38,
        106
instrument 62, 66
    three-stringed 66
    two-stringed 64
intention 4-6, 10, 14, 15, 32, 33, 127
internal variable 105, 106, 108, 111,
    115-117, 121, 131, 132, 134
interval 1, 2, 18, 19, 23, 57-68, 70,
    72-78, 94, 98, 99
    elite 65, 66, 69-73, 75-78
    superelite 68, 73
intonation 62
Just Intonation 2, 57, 58-60, 64, 65,
    68, 72
law
    generalized matching 112
    matching iii, 105, 107,
        110-114, 118, 119, 129, 135
    rational 1, 26, 89
    of Effect 110, 136
    of Internality 109-111
    of Reflex 108, 110
law of conditional and unconditional
    Reflex 109, 110
magnitude estimation 21, 22, 27, 89

major
    profiles of 69, 71
    triads 68, 69
mental activity 107
mentalism 105
mere exposure 43, 44, 96, 102
minor
    profiles of 69, 71
    triads 68, 69
moral 4, 21, 103, 126, 128, 134
    choice 4, 106, 109, 136
    judgment 41, 99
musical zones 62-64, 77, 78, 95
patterns
    Baum's 112, 125
    behavioral 113, 122, 127
Pelog 58, 59, 63, 64, 72, 73
polarity 103, 122
pole
    belief 37, 38, 41, 43, 45, 50, 51
    negative 1, 3, 4, 16, 29, 47, 81, 106, 108, 115, 118, 125, 131
    positive 3, 4, 9, 14, 16, 29, 32, 34, 35, 47, 48, 81, 106, 108, 115, 118, 119, 121-127, 131
preferences 32, 61, 94, 96, 98, 100, 101, 109, 126, 127, 134
probability
    downloading of 107, 108, 109
    traces of 119
projection 1, 17, 18, 25, 37, 42, 44, 55, 64, 65, 74
purity 134
Pythagorean tuning 57, 58
readiness 4-6, 9, 10, 14, 16, 32-35, 38, 81, 103

reflex 109, 136
    conditional 110
    unconditional 110
sacred shift 128
screen 1, 16-19, 21, 24, 29, 37, 38, 41-43, 45, 64, 74
self 13, 37, 47, 50, 52, 65, 73, 93, 98, 105, 107, 122, 126, 127, 129
    image of 1, 3, 8-10, 13-15, 32, 81, 83, 84, 87
    model of 13, 14, 84
    trend to 16, 32, 33
self-evaluation 48-52
self-reflexion 13, 96, 136
social choice 38
star's brightness 27
state 1, 4, 16-18, 31, 33, 37, 42-44, 55, 64, 65, 73-75, 88, 90, 118, 119
    emotional 64, 73, 74
    mixed 16-18, 25, 38, 41, 107, 108, 119, 121, 128
    pure 17, 107
    uncertain 17, 107, 121, 122
subject
    algebraic 87
    autonomous 31-35, 37, 42, 44, 55, 65
    with internality 105, 108, 114, 119, 120
trend 13, 32
    the self 16, 32, 33
    an external object 15, 33, 35
two-hump distribution 42
utility-measure 114, 127, 134